PASSIVE INCOME BLUEPRINT

A Comprehensive Guide to a
Definite 6-Figure Cash Flow

By

Brett Smith

First Edition 2018

Copyright – Brett Smith

All rights reserved.

No part of this publication may be reproduced, stored in or introduced into a retrieval system, or transmitted in any form, or by any means (electronic, mechanical, photocopying, recording or otherwise) without the prior written permission of the author.

This book is sold subject to the condition that is shall not, by way of trade or otherwise, be lent, resold, hired out or otherwise circulated without the author's prior consent in any form of binding or cover other than that in which it is published and without a similar condition including this condition being imposed on the subsequent purchaser.

Introduction

Make as much money as you want, and live the life you damn well please!

Ask any hundred individuals whether they are committed with expanding their wealth and each of them will say yes. However, ask them whether they are 'not kidding' about it, about half will shrug. Hell, many people are not even 'genuine' about their well-being, not to mention their wealth, but it's those individuals who are really dedicated to activity that have a real effect in their own lives. The real difference between the wealthy and the poor is that wealthy individuals make a move (since they are focused on their wealth), while the poor are individuals who tend to consider change, but seldom take the activities important to make it.

If you are not kidding about expanding your wealth, at that point you will need to pursue this book, since it is the beginning stage – this is the place everything gets intense, and where change will pursue.

So you are committed, isn't that so? Since regardless you understanding, you should be.

A number of individuals have known about 'passive income' but not many completely comprehend what it implies. Passive income is characterized as income that you do not need to work for. As it were, if you are on a radiant shoreline traveling with your family, you can even now be gaining cash. The way to creating progressing and developing wealth is to work for passive income, rather than working income.

For instance, if you are a Doctor, Lawyer, Waiter or Astronaut, when you quit working, you profit. Your working income is no more. You may have a lot of cash, but you don't make more except if you put on your work garments, get in the auto, and go to work. The rich tend to center around winning passive income rather, with the goal that their wealth develops every day, regardless of whether they go to work or go to the Riviera to take a shot at their tan. In addition, that is the reason the rich continue getting more extravagant while every other person gets poorer. Also, poorer. What's more, poorer.

Reasonable cautioning! Do not surmise that building passive income is simple – it is definitely not. It takes some work to set up your base, and it takes arranging and duty to manufacture that base, and except if you construct your base, that passive income will never come.

How about we consider it another way – you could burn through 40 hours this week working for an insurance agency as an office representative, and you'll just make $10 or $12 a hour toward its finish. But burn through 40 hours chipping away at building your passive income and you can get that $10 or $12 (or a whole lot more) coming in throughout the day, consistently - even on weekends!

Imagine earning $400 before you even get up toward the beginning of the day. Imagine earning $50 as you have breakfast. Imagine going on siestas for a week and getting back home to discover a check for $5,000 via the post office. That is passive income.

So how might you get this going? All things considered, stage one is to not stop your normal everyday employment, as it will take some work before you can live off of your passive income and quit the 9 to5. Building passive income is long haul thinking – not here and now, so meanwhile you have to keep your bills paid. However, recall, the wealthy are those that make a move. The poor are those that return home from work and 'turn off'.

Real Estate is a standout among other approaches to accomplish passive income. For instance, if you purchase a decent property or business building and rent it out, and your home loan installments are not as much as the lease you get, at that point you have quite recently created a passive income. The huge issue is, obviously, that a great many people do not have the huge measures of capital required to purchase real estate. Therefore, you may need to bring down your sights a little to approaches to make smaller measures of passive income, with a significantly smaller venture, so you can work your way up to property speculation later.

MLM, or Multi-level Marketing, has for some time been a wellspring of passive income for individuals that don't have the enormous cash to contribute forthright, and keeping in mind that a few people timid far from MLM frameworks, you should comprehend before going in that the manner in which they work isn't care for it is in the infomercials. You do not simply join a MLM framework and in a flash begin making hundreds of thousands of dollars – you need to work at it. If you know anybody that has become famous in whenever of MLM business at that point chances are they placed in long hard hours offering. This is a noteworthy drawback since a great many people do not care for offering. The ideal approach to produce passive income is to locate a real business that requires no offering.

However, there are successful businesses out there that will produce a reliable and solid passive income without the problem of offering, and without hundreds of thousands of dollars expected to get in on the ground floor. If you are focused on making passive income for you and your family, and need to begin small and construct a solid base.

Keep in mind – the wealthy take action. If you are not kidding about expanding your wealth, you will as well.

A note from the author…

This book contains a step-by-step guide with tons of valuable information that will help you to create a 6-figure passive cash flow. This comprehensive guide has helped me and more than 50 of my students to create successful passive businesses that allow us to experience the amazing life that we live today. Hopefully, you will be the next one to join us.

However, keep in mind that just by reading this book, money is not going to fall from the sky through the roof on to your table. To be successful financially, work is required. No one is successful at anything in the world without taking action and put in the work that is required.

Creating a passive income flow is all about creating a automated business that runs without consuming your time and effort. To get to that point, you are going to need to put in the hours that are required initially. If you do so, you will be rewarded with awesome results.

Creating a successful passive business is about having the right mindset towards it too. Persistence, consistency and the rock solid mindset are the basic requirements.

In order to get the maximum value out of this book, get a pen and a note book alongside with you. Turn on your computer and get prepared. Whenever you get a new idea, jot it down and implement it right away. Speed of implantation equals speed of success. Procrastination is for children.

Table of Contents

Chapter 1:

Complete Clickbank Guide ……………...………….. *page 09*

Chapter 2:

Incredible Traffic Wave …….. *page 52*

Chapter 3:

Affiliate Marketing Super Shot ………………………….. *page 93*

Chapter 4:

The Most Brilliant Marketing Strategies ……………. *page 100*

Chapter 5:

Benefiting from the Impressive Google AdSense World

……..…… *page 178*

The Gift Package ………………………………….....…… *page 266*

Chapter 1

Complete Clickbank Guide

What Is Clickbank?

If you are an entrepreneur, at that point you may have known about Clickbank, particularly if you are building up your business on the web. If you are new to the universe of web based marketing and strategies, Clickbank is a perfect place to begin. To put it plainly, you can begin a business inside a couple of minutes by offering not your own items but rather those of others on the web. You don't must have an item to offer, a business to advance or even have any thought what you might want to do. Clickbank offers a lot of alternatives for everybody.

Things being what they are, What Is It?

The organization came to be in 1998. It considers itself a protected, online retail outlet. There are thousands of items available to be purchased at the site whenever. As of now, there are in excess of 12,000 advanced item sellers at the site. For those 12,000 items, there are in excess of 100,000 dynamic member advertisers. This vast number of associate advertisers ought not appear to be overwhelming. In spite of the fact that they are your opposition as an online entrepreneur, there are such huge numbers of incredible items, a considerable lot of them new constantly, being added to Clickbank that you can depend on having a decent enthusiasm for the items you offer yourself, even with that measure of rivalry.

The organization is noteworthy. For instance, at regular intervals, some place on the planet there is a deal being made. If you factor that out, it goes to nearly 26,000 advanced exchanges for every day. That is outstanding. In addition, if you choose to work with Clickbank, your market is huge. The organization gives administrations to those in excess of 200 nations. Contemplating this, you may think about whether there are items accessible to fill those demands. The appropriate response is yes. All the more in this way, if you factor in the way that Clickbank is additionally a standout amongst the most very positioned sites for movement on an everyday schedule, that excessively demonstrates the power behind this organization.

If you are new to web based marketing or are searching for extraordinary items to offer, fortunately you will discover the choices you require at Clickbank. All the more along these lines, the reasonableness and the devices that the organization gives to clients additionally empower individuals to profit by this administration. You don't have to put excessively time and cash into the procedure to begin. Or maybe, investigate what is accessible at the site. It is sufficient to get generally charmed.

Why Become an Affiliate Through Clickbank?

As you consider beginning another business from home, you may have kept running into the open doors that exist through Clickbank, an organization that connections the advertiser to the item maker, and handles everything in the middle of for the two gatherings. There is something said in regards to being a maker or seller of your own item. Be that as it may, it takes a lot of time and exertion to plan these items. At that point, to get them online can be troublesome. If you need an extraordinary method to profit and would prefer not to make your very own item, at that point going the course of being a Clickbank partner might be the best alternative for you.

What are the advantages of being a Clickbank subsidiary, rather than working with different organizations or even with the item maker all alone?

With Clickbank, you can procure as much as 75 percent commission on your deals.

That is a sizable measure of cash thinking of you as did not make the item yourself. Obviously, it is critical to take note of that not all Clickbank items do in truth offer the 75 percent commission, but numerous a greater amount of them do contrast with different items out there.

You can choose from 12,000 different items to advance. Else, you would be constrained by the choices accessible to you. That won't assist you with turning the benefit you need to. You can consolidate your profit if you work with Clickbank. The organization is intended to gather the installment specifically from the client who makes the buy. The merchant handles the distribution, but Clickbank almost requires the conveyance of such items to be prompt. Clickbank gathers the majority of the assets from the majority of the advancements you go up against and then pays you for them on a week after week premise.

You additionally get incredible following and installment frameworks through Clickbank. Discover what is offering, how it is offering and decides whether you have to roll out any improvements to the procedure.

As you can envision, it is very productive to work with Clickbank for the majority of your needs. As a member advertiser, you need to have the most items to look over as could be expected under the circumstances. You likewise need to be able to depend on installment, as opposed to hold up for somebody to pay you. There are numerous motivations to work with Clickbank but filling in as an associate is a standout amongst other choices around.

What Products Are Allowed At Clickbank?

Clickbank is a significant extensive organization and they are boundless in what kinds of items you can offer at their site. In any case, there are confinements that you should think about before you join at Clickbank. The organization enables you to list a huge assortment of items, but those items must meet some specific criteria with the end goal to go on the site. Take a gander at what the organization considers the must have list.

The Product Needs To Be Original

The fundamental thought for any item that you list on Clickbank is that it must be a unique item. That is, it must be your own, or you should possess the lawful rights to offer it. The item must be unique or have the vital licenses for you to offer it. You can't, in any capacity encroach on the licensed innovation of others utilizing the Clickbank benefit. For whatever length of time that you possess every one of the rights to the material, and nobody else does, you ought to have the capacity to show it on Clickbank as an unique item.

It Must Digitally Delivered

The item must have the capacity to have conveyance from you to the client carefully. This implies the item should be sold in at least one organizations that enable clients to download or acquire access to the data. The most well-known strategies for doing this are to utilize website pages, messages sent inside 24 hours of the buy and through downloadable documents. The organization requests that you furnish the client with the capacity to acquire quickly his or her item, so quick conveyance is a smart thought. Regardless, you do need to tell your client, before their buy of the item, when you will convey it to them, and how you will do as such. A few things, called supplemental material, might be delivered to the client. For instance, this may incorporate precedent books, DVD's or CD's. It is conceivable to utilize Clickbank to send this data but the item they get along these lines ought to be complimentary and not basic data to the next item they purchase through the site and acquire carefully. In other words, you have to give an advanced item but anything additional can ship to them as printed media.

Understanding the items and administrations that Clickbank permits is an imperative procedure to understanding if the item you are offering will function admirably there.

Clearing Up Questions About Clickbank

As any great advanced item proprietor would do, you may have a few inquiries regarding utilizing Clickbank for your item. There are questions that multiple occasions can be facilitated by realizing that others are doing with the administration. Then again, you might need to know why Clickbank is preferable for you over another administration that is out there. Fortunately much of the time, this organization works to perfection of getting your item out there and helping you to advance it.

Does Clickbank set the cost for my item? One of the greatest misinterpretations is that Clickbank reveals to you what to value your item at. This isn't valid. Truth be told, Clickbank is an incredible place to go to discover data and rules for evaluating your item. You can contrast what your item offers with what the other person's does and then value it as needs be.

Does Clickbank reveal to me the amount to pay subsidiaries? At the point when your item is recorded at Clickbank with the goal that partners can marketing it for you, you get the chance to set the associate offer. This is the measure of commission the member gets for offering your item. Once more, utilize the administrations at the site to assist you with getting a thought of what the others are offering items like your very own with.

Is there a continuous charge Clickbank makes you pay? There is an expense you do need to pay to utilize Clickbank called an initiation charge. This charge isn't intended to be continuous, but an onetime installment to the administration to get your computerized item on the web. In any case, you may need to pay this charge more than once if you have in excess of one item you need to list at the site.

Additionally, it is imperative to take note of that numerous individuals stress that utilizing administrations like this is simply too difficult to do. You might be stressed that the administration will be difficult to use in your site or that you might be not able work through the set up process without anyone else. This is understandable but Clickbank offers an answer. Their client benefit is perfect and it will furnish you with the majority of the data and assets you have to get your item online effectively. You don't must have a great deal of involvement to discover the procedure simple to oversee alone.

Tips For Promoting Your Clickbank Affiliation

As there are numerous approaches to construct a business on the web, there are similarly the same number of approaches to advance your subsidiary item from Clickbank. When you join with a record for Clickbank, the subsequent stage in the process is to acquire a hoplink. This straightforward URL is related with you and your Clickbank account. At whatever point anybody taps on that connection, they will be taken to the buy site to purchase the item, but in light of the fact that they have utilized your connection, you will get kudos for the deal.

Getting acknowledgment for the deal implies commission winds up in your pocket. In spite of the fact that this is something worth being thankful for, the crucial step is inspiring individuals to tap on your connection. The accompanying tips will assist you with promoting your member connection and item.

Make a site devoted to your Clickbank advancement. This site ought to be data, deals or a blend. The objective here is to tell others about the item and then to fuse your hoplink into that site and direct the activity to the pages to make their buy.

You can make an email battle by incorporating joins in the messages that you convey to leads. It is vital to have just gotten the leads in a proper way; nonetheless, it is a smart thought to utilize an email crusade for the individuals who visit your site. They may not purchase the item immediately, but rather you can inspire them to return to your site on numerous occasions through an email crusade.

You can likewise advance your hoplink through social marketing. This more up to date sort of marketing is truly outstanding in the present market. The objective is to speak with others about your item and administration through social sites like Facebook, Myspace or others. At that point, make certain to incorporate your hoplink in the majority of the messages that you convey.

Advancing your offshoot marketing can get unpredictable, but once you begin with these essential apparatuses, whatever remains of the procedure is simpler. The better you are at advancing your item, the higher your benefit potential will be. Most organizations will discover those strategies for advancement that work best for them, and for their item. It takes just a couple of minutes for you to make a hoplink for an item at Clickbank. From that point, the advancement of that connection is in your hands, however you do need to keep it spam free.

Tips For Making Your Affiliate Business With Clickbank Successful

With the end goal to be fruitful as an associate advertiser with your Clickbank items, you have to know how to advance your item. You ought to have invested some energy examining the items that were accessible with the goal that you have an important and exceptionally helpful item to offer. You ought to have chosen an item that offers a decent level of commission, with the goal that you can make sure that there is a benefit to be made here. In view of that, consider the accompanying strategies for

advancing your Clickbank item.

Tips for Promotional Success

The accompanying advances can assist you with promoting your Clickbank item, without squandering your time.

Set up a blog. A blog is the best alternative for most organizations since it enables your business to develop and thrive on the web. It likewise enables you to add consistent substance to your site, which will assist you with ranking admirably in web indexes.

Do some watchword examine. You have to comprehend what words individuals are composing into web indexes to discover your site or sites like your own. There are free administrations that make this procedure.

Utilize watchwords in your space name, labels, features, and in the substance on your site.

This data will assist you with improving your general outcomes since it is the thing that web crawlers are searching for to rank sites appropriately.

Put resources into article marketing. Compose articles about your item or administration and post them on article registries. You would then be able to utilize this data to pipe more business from those indexes to your site. Along these lines, you have profoundly focused on leads coming into your business.

Do put resources into social marketing strategies. Social marketing enables you to converse with others about your item and business and along these lines to get them intrigued. You can utilize any number of the social marketing sites, similar to Twitter, Facebook, Digg and MySpace to assist you with this procedure. Research demonstrates the individuals who react to promotions through online life will probably purchase.

When you pull the majority of this together, the way toward making an extraordinary site is simple enough to do. Remember the significance of giving educational data and following any confinements that Clickbank may put on you. You need to guarantee that you are not doing anything that is spam. When you work your business through these advancement strategies, you will begin to see benefits coming in from Clickbank.

Utilizing Search Engine Marketing For Your Clickbank Hoplink

Web index marketing is a standout amongst the most vital techniques for marketing any business on the web. The objective of marketing in the web indexes is very basic. You need the web search tools, similar to Google and Yahoo to put your site or blog at the highest priority on their rundown. When somebody composes in a watchword that fits the item you are offering, you need your site to be at the highest priority on the rundown of results. The higher it is in this rundown, the better your odds of getting individuals to your site where you can pitch the item to them.

Making great internet searcher marketing can be mind boggling and some partner advertisers really procure experts to do this work for them. It is a smart thought to advance your associate items in this way, particularly when you combine it with other limited time techniques. Here are a few hints to assist you with web crawler marketing.

Do explore on watchwords, or words that individuals will probably type into web crawlers to discover your site or sites like your own. You can utilize an assortment of online administrations to assist you with finding the correct catchphrases for your subject. They are allowed to utilize.

Make certain that your site's area name and labels all contain these catchphrases. You need the web indexes to realize that you are not kidding about your item and that your site is the best site for that item. Something else, different sites will be set before your own, cutting into your benefits.

Utilize watchwords in your general site content. Use a blog and make certain to incorporate catchphrases in those blog entries. Fuse titles and pages of your site remembering the watchwords.

Do give quality data. If you pack your site brimming with an excessive number of catchphrases or squandered data, you won't get great outcomes from any web crawlers. Likewise, web crawlers will punish your site for abuse.

Keep new substance coming. Make sure to post to your blog once a day. Stay aware of new substance for the site.

When you consolidate these techniques into your special procedure for your Clickbank hoplink, you will see more outcomes. This implies more deals for you and more benefits for your pockets. Internet searcher marketing is one a player in an intricate strategy for advancing your Clickbank items appropriately.

The Problem With Pricing Your Clickbank Product Too Low

You may never have suspected that you could value your Clickbank item too low. It occurs and regularly it happens to the death of the item. If you know you have a quality item and you realize that what that item contains will in certainty help other people, at that point in all likelihood it is a smart thought for you to value that item sufficiently high. As you consider the majority of the estimating alternatives for a Clickbank item, don't value your item too low. It could moderate your deals excessively.

The drawback to estimating your Clickbank item too low is that it might in certainty cause various clients, and members, not to try and notice it. Set aside the opportunity to figure out what the correct cost for your item depends on esteem and rivalry, not only a low number.

There are a couple of things to consider here. You might be astonished to realize that a few items flop on Clickbank on the grounds that they are estimated too low!

The most ideal approach to drive deals to your Clickbank item isn't to value it low, but rather to value it comfortable esteem. This will help support deals since individuals will realize that the item you are putting forth is high in esteem. Individuals need to purchase esteem not simply gibberish data that is useless to them. They liken a modest cost with a modest item.

Additionally remember that all together for your item to do well on Clickbank, you have to guarantee that there are partners who will advance that item for you. If you value it too low, the measure of commission that a subsidiary may gain is too low to turn a benefit. This wards off them, which implies lost deals for your item.

Regardless of whether you do cost your item low and do see deals increment, this does not mean it is the correct cost for your item. If just 10 members will advance your item in light of its low cost, and you influence 100 deals, to envision what might occur if 20 partners sold your item at a marginally higher cost.

As should be obvious, valuing your Clickbank item too low could make you lose business instead of make business. Clickbank offers devices to assist you with pricing it right. Set aside the opportunity to think about them before putting a number on it.

The Problem With Pricing Your Clickbank Product Too High

Estimating your Clickbank item without flaw will transform your item into a benefit creator. Value your item too low and you will wind up confronting a sizable loss of benefit. In the meantime, you do need to settle that your item may not be the $1000 item you thought it was. That does not mean it can't turn a benefit for you. Actually, if you center around getting your cost in that sweet spot, odds are great you will discover genuine benefit from those deals. Is your Clickbank item excessively costly?

For what reason do a few people on Clickbank escape with valuing their item so high and as yet having various associates to advance that item? Keep in mind, the way to progress on Clickbank is to list your item at the correct cost. If the cost is too low, you won't draw in enough members to do the advancement work that you require them to do. Then again, if you value that item too high, you won't have the clients to purchase from you, regardless of whether you have an extensive number of partner advertisers advancing the item. Thus, at that point, the inquiry remains, how do a few people offer so well at such a higher value point?

The greater part of the individuals who have items that are offering admirably on Clickbank at a higher rate than normal are for the most part the entrenched experts. They have typically sold various different books or items along these lines and have built up a solid notoriety for themselves. As it were, partner advertisers realize that what that individual is offering will perform well in the commercial center, maybe on the grounds that past items did well. This drives the estimation of the item higher and makes more demand in the commercial center for it.

If you are simply beginning, estimating your item too high won't assist you with making more cash. Or maybe, it might drive away the potential clients that you require with the end goal to pitch enough items to make a benefit. What's more, Clickbank regularly cautions that if you value your item too high and the client feels that it does not merit the value, this could prompt higher quantities of discounts, which frighten away partner advertisers. Get the value right, however, and you will offer the high number of items you are seeking after, and still turn a decent item in volume of offers.

Offshoots Do Not Deliver With Clickbank Products

There are numerous motivations to begin your very own online business, but a standout amongst the most essential to recollect is that you can do advancing other individuals' items and not need to stress over the real item itself. If you work through Clickbank, for instance, as an offshoot advertiser, you can offer and advance items that others make. You get the opportunity to acquire a sizable commission for giving this administration, as well. This has been a strategy that many have used to turn benefits consistently. Is it appropriate for you?

One of the hang ups numerous individuals have with regards to beginning their own online business is their absence of capacity to understand that they don't must have a distribution center brimming with merchandise to pitch to clients. For instance, you don't must have your home's carport supplied up with pooch items to offer canine items. If you are an associate for a maker or seller, as they are called, at that point your activity is to just set up the site, advance the item and then let the seller handle whatever remains of the work for you.

How does this function? Consider how it functions at Clickbank, an administration that is intended to make the activity of an associate unfathomably simple.

You agree to accept a free record with Clickbank. You make a one of a kind URL called a hoplink that identifies only you, after you have chosen an item to advance through their administration.

You make a blog or utilize different techniques to advance the item. Inside the substance of any limited time component you make, you additionally incorporate that hoplink that Clickbank gave to you.

At whatever point somebody goes to your substance, peruses your limited time substance and taps on your connection, they are taken to the Clickbank account or to a pitch page where there is more data and the assets for paying for the item. They get it.

Clickbank handles the installment preparing, sending your bonus straightforwardly to your record. The seller handles the conveyance of the item to the client, for the most part on a moment premise.

As should be obvious by this precedent, you don't need to stress over the procedure. The computerized items convey right away and that implies quicker commissions for you. Not at all like different items out there, Clickbank makes it simple for a partner to turn a benefit utilizing their administration.

Clickbank Gets Your Digital Product Online

For the individuals who are makers of advanced items, for example, eBooks, the hardest part to profiting from them is getting them into the hands of the individuals who can and will purchase the book. Sites are a basic part of this. Having a blog, doing some interpersonal interaction and notwithstanding handling a couple of requests all over is a decent begin, but most computerized item makers require more than this if they would like to do well in the business. To get to the following level, consider using the administrations of Clickbank.

How Can It Work

Make your advanced item. For instance, if you are energetic about carpentry, make an eBook that furnishes others with the learning that you have. That digital book can be evaluated as you might want to. It is a smart thought to inquire about the best costs for books like your own, in view of the current going rate for items like yours. Clickbank can assist you with this kind of research if you are uncertain how to value the book. With the book in hand, the subsequent stage is to set up your site so you can begin pulling in guests to it. Clickbank can likewise assist you with the installment preparing and extortion security that you require. This empowers you to get your item on the web.

Advancement Through Affiliates

The subsequent stage in getting your advanced item before the majority is to permit Clickbank's mass of 100,000-subsidiary advertisers offer your eBook for you. These experts can help you by advancing your book for you. They get a charge from the book's deals, each time they offer one. Be that as it may, in light of the fact that there are such a large number of who are probably going to get your book and advance it, it is likewise likely that you will see generous development in deals. Rather than offering 10 books for every month through your site, you could be offering that numerous every day, or more, contingent upon the market for your item.

As should be obvious, it is astute to put your time in working with Clickbank if you are a computerized item proprietor or might want to be. If you have data and information to impart to the world that you believe is significant, make an eBook or other advanced item and use the assets that Clickbank offers to get your book before those that are probably going to have the capacity to enable you to make it productive.

Clickbank Pricing: High Prices for High Value

With regards to estimating your Clickbank item, it is imperative for you to think about the estimation of the item. To put it plainly, you need to guarantee that your item has the estimation of the value point. When you do some essential research on your item, contrasted with others available, you will have an unmistakable thought of what a decent value point will be. Be that as it may, you do need to factor in the estimation of your item contrasted with their item.

One error a few people make is posting their item at indistinguishable cost from every other person's without considering what the other person is really advertising. If you have an item that offers genuine incentive to the purchaser, at that point you should set a higher cost for it. Try not to be reluctant to value your item higher if you realize that what you are putting forth is in certainty a superior item than the other person.

For instance, let us expect that you are offering an eBook on getting a good deal on offering your home. You are likely offering great data and maybe unique data. You realize that what is in the other person's eBook isn't close at all to what you are putting into your item. You could be sparing the client thousands of dollars. Your book may then be worth more than the other person. If their item is estimated at $20, but you know your incentive far surpasses this, value yours at $50.

If you do list your item at a higher value point since you know the esteem is higher, it will be vital for you to demonstrate to your client (and to the offshoots who will advertise your book) that the esteem is there. This may take all the more arranging and association. You should show the genuine estimation of the book somehow. When you agree to accept Clickbank, you will finish a page called a Pitch Page, or, in other words will portray the item in detail to persuade your associates to go up against your item. This is the place you should prevail upon them.

Estimating your Clickbank item legitimately is very basic. Without the correct value, you won't profit. If your item is of a high esteem, at that point value it to coordinate that high esteem. It will, at last, kill a few, but it will turn greater benefits for you if it merits the cash.

Clickbank Pricing Experiments Are Important

There are numerous things to consider when evaluating your Clickbank items. A unique little something is the estimation of your item contrasted with others. Another is the present ordinary rate for items like your own. Shockingly, there is no real way to tell if your item will offer well at some cost. Therefore, one of the means in posting your item on Clickbank is to explore different avenues regarding the cost. At the end of the day, there might be the need to change out the cost every once in a while to all the more likely mirror the commercial center.

A standout amongst other approaches to try different things with your item on Clickbank is to exploit the capacity you need to offer numerous renditions of your item through a solitary Clickbank account. What does that mean? For one, you can utilize it to offer your item at different value focuses. Thusly, you can figure out which cost is the best one for the best deals and benefit. In any case, you should demonstrate that there is some difference in one form of your item than the other, but this can be as simple as offering rewards or broadened variants.

For what reason would it matter, you may inquire. Once in a while, the cost of your item will impact the business you will or won't have. For instance, if you value your item too low, you may make an picture with your offshoots and clients that the item isn't profitable. Then again, you may value it too high, which may influence it to appear to be unrealistic. Try not to expect that a lower cost is continually going to be the correct alternative. Or maybe, utilize a touch of testing to figure out which cost is the correct ones for you.

A marginally higher cost may urge more deals associates to work with you. You may influence your item to appear to be more important to the client. This may transform into more deals for you. The key is to return to that value point a few times and question if it is the correct one. Since you can list your item at different value focuses, fortunately you can almost certainly dismiss a benefit right. You can see the difference the value difference makes immediately with these numerous records. Analyze and change your cost as fundamental. You can transform it whenever much of the time.

Reoccurring or Subscription Products on Clickbank

Wouldn't it be something worth being thankful for to have the capacity to pull in clients back to your item over and over and to gather another expense for doing as such? This is something you can do. Huge numbers of the most gainful online business experts are utilizing Clickbank to make reoccurring or membership administrations or items. The decent thing about such an open door is, to the point that it makes a constant flow of pay for you, accepting that you plan the item appropriately and have enough recruits to prop it up.

What Is A Reoccurring Subscription?

When you utilize Clickbank to make a reoccurring deal or membership benefit, you consider the organization to take mechanized installments from the client on a set calendar. For instance, let us say that you are offering an educational book on system marketing. As a feature of a continuous administration, you might want to offer the customer 100 leads for each month for a set expense. Your offshoots advance this administration. Your clients buy the administration, knowing completely that they are purchasing a membership of leads. Every month, on the date assigned, Clickbank will process the installment for the leads for you and the leads are naturally sent to your endorser, through your framework.

The framework that Clickbank offers is completely mechanized. This implies the advancing, offering and administration of the exchanges is improved the situation you, without you getting engaged with the procedure other than satisfying your client's requests, sometimes.

When you set up a membership benefit this way, you enable your clients to purchase something from you consistently. This might be as straightforward as paying for a product permit or something more broad, for example, approaching an enrollment site. The key here is that the client needs to get something of significant worth on a progressing reason for you to utilize membership administrations like this.

Fortunately when you utilize Clickbank to do this, you are really ready to set up an administration that is powerful and furnishes you with the best capacity for your framework. You can pick how frequently the framework forms installment. You can pick how the item functions. Much the same as some other item you offer on Clickbank, you set the costs and pick the conveyance strategy. The difference is that this time, the buys will be progressing instead of an onetime arrangement you make with the client.

Clickbank Prohibited Items

As you consider getting your item recorded on Clickbank, take note of that a few things are restricted by the organization. At the end of the day, if your item falls under one of these classes, it will be not able have a posting on the site as a subsidiary item. Lamentably, this rundown is to some degree broad. In any case, most items and administrations that you may bring to the table are in reality going to be permitted. The organization has to restrict the sorts of items permitted simply because some might be impolite or possibly illicit or hurtful.

What Is Limited?

A fairly full rundown of things is denied from being incorporated into Clickbank. This rundown likewise changes, which implies that you should look at it frequently to guarantee your item is still permitted on the site.

Maybe the biggest measure of substance not permitted is anything that is unlicensed restrictive substance. At the end of the day, except if you have the privilege to offer the item, don't attempt to offer it. Likewise, remember that Clickbank holds the sole appropriate to condemn the item. If they find that anything is unlawful or accept than any data is wrong for the site, they have the privilege to point of confinement or boycott the data.

Different items that can't be incorporated into Clickbank items incorporate the accompanying:

No spyware compose items or material examining this item in a positive light.

Existing promissory notes or obligations

Advanced money may not be incorporated

Deeds or titles

Lottery tickets or any sort of sweepstakes

Erotic entertainment

Warez

Spending accounts

Workshop or different sorts of tickets

Standardized savings numbers or queries

Counterfeit identification apparatuses

Apparatuses for spamming

Items that are advertised through Craigslist

Secret word records

This rundown proceeds. If you are uncertain if your item might be allowable to the Clickbank item bank, it is dependably a smart thought to call them or send off an email. Client bolster is very compelling, and will answer your inquiries speedily. You can likewise look for updates on new items that might be disallowed by watching the organization's site or blog. As a rule, however, the item you are offering will be admissible on the grounds that it is a lawful item to offer. For whatever length of time that you claim the rights and the material is totally ok, you ought to have no issue!

Clickbank Variety Helps Affiliates

The individuals who need to seek after a member vocation on the web, and turn some genuine benefits, can do as such through the Clickbank benefit. This organization can unite the seller or maker of the item and the general population who will advance and offer it. This is an outstanding relationship in light of the fact that Clickbank handles the exchanges, to guarantee that everybody gets what they have to without stressing over the cash part of it. One of alternate advantages of utilizing Clickbank as an associate is the way that you can pick between a huge number of items to offer.

Items Offered By Clickbank

As you agree to accept a free record with Clickbank, you will access the organization's enormous rundown of offshoot items, all of which you can choose from and advance as you might want to. You can begin your advancements immediately. There is no endorsement procedure you need to experience to begin the procedure. Nonetheless, you would prefer only not to bounce on any item that you find that looks intriguing. Get your work done and some exploration to locate the correct item for your specific needs. This will enhance your odds of offering an item you can be glad for.

Remember that the expansive assortment of items on Clickbank does not imply that each one of those items is a decent decision for associates. Some offer higher commissions, but might be harder to offer. Others are valued so low that you can't generally divert a tolerable commission from them. The best items are discovered some place in the center here. It is dependent upon you to discover the item that is appropriate for you and to decide the correct method to advance it. There are a few advantages of working with Clickbank, however.

With such a large number of items to choose from, it is conceivable to discover items not oversaturated in the commercial center to advance.

You can begin advancing your item immediately. You don't have to sit tight for endorsement from the seller or maker.

There are no individual contracts required to offer the items on Clickbank. This makes it simple to kick the procedure off immediately.

Clickbank professes to be the biggest commercial center holder for subsidiary advertisers. Fortunately the organization offers various choices in for all intents and purposes each specialty. This is an incredible place to discover the item you need to offer.

Simple Commerce Benefits Of Clickbank

There are numerous motivations to swing to Clickbank. For the individuals who are searching for an approach to profit on the web, Clickbank gives that alternative to you. Maybe you are somebody who has made your very own computerized item. You have made a site, but you are not seeing the development that you sought after. Before surrendering, it is astute to swing to Clickbank, or another site like it,

and use the administrations offered to you there to turn a benefit. Fortunately you ought to have the capacity to get results regardless of what kind or specialty you are in.

Specifically, however, a considerable lot of the advantages of Clickbank originate from the simple trade structure. These apparatuses have a plan to make your activity as simple as could be expected under the circumstances. In any case, would could it be that Clickbank offers to clients?

1. Clickbank furnishes clients with an extremely straightforward, secure and solid strategy for preparing installment. If you don't know how you will process installments on your site, remove the difficulty from the procedure and swing it to Clickbank.

2. There are low expenses related with setting up your Clickbank account. The charges for actuation of your item on the site are one-time expenses. This expense enables you to access the instruments and administrations accessible, and to the bigger commercial center to impart your item to.

3. You can acknowledge charge cards, PayPal installments and different types of installment through your Clickbank account. This enables your shoppers to have the choices they have to purchase from you.

4. You don't need to make a shipper record to set up your Clickbank account. This implies you don't need to stress over those additional expenses or related concerns.

5. You get top quality extortion insurance from Clickbank. This secures your item, your budgetary data and even your installments. You can't do that through your own site, much of the time.

One more of the additional advantages of utilizing Clickbank for your trade needs is the client support and administration. The organization guides you through the procedure and empowers you to have the assets and instruments you have to get your business off the ground rapidly. Regardless of whether you are as of now internet, doing not too bad business, you may require an administration like what is offered by Clickbank to get your business to the following level. It is certainly justified regardless of the venture for generally organizations.

Finding A Product To Promote From Clickbank

Make a stride back and understand that you have the chance to advance items on the web, without taking care of the cash and the conveyance procedure of those items. You have these advantages if you choose to utilize Clickbank to encourage you. There are various items out there and administrations intended to furnish offshoots with the assets they have to advance items, but Clickbank offers a few favorable circumstances. One of those favorable circumstances is the way that you have such a significant number of items to offer through Clickbank.

Subsequent to setting up a record with Clickbank, you will approach the Market Place. This is where the majority of the Clickbank items are found. You can without much of a stretch experience the a huge number of items and figure out which the correct one is for you. Be that as it may, usually a superior alternative to contribute somewhat more time and to do some exploration on the items accessible. The accompanying tips will help you through the procedure.

Do some fundamental catchphrase explore. You are probably going to utilize watchwords to advance your member items and in this way it is imperative to know how well the item is set up to accommodate catchphrases.

Do some essential research on the item itself. Does the item offer something really novel? It is vital to have a full handle of what the item is and what it offers before you choose to advance it.

Is this item estimated right? There are two things to consider here. If it is estimated low, odds are great your member bonus will likewise be low. That isn't what you need. Then again, if it is too high, this could make you lose deals in light of the fact that customers might not have any desire to contribute as much as the cost recorded. Searching at the correct cost is imperative.

Look at the opposition. Those offshoot items that have a lot of other offshoots elevating it are probably not going to furnish you with the assets you need and need. Or maybe, it is imperative for you to choose an item that has less rivalry and a less soaked market.

Doing some homework at the Clickbank Market Place will assist you with improving your odds of getting incredible deals. Remember that not all items will turn the outcomes you need, but the more research you do now the happier your will be benefit astute.

The Benefits of a Clickbank Subscription Product

Having a reoccurring membership item through Clickbank could be extraordinary compared to other choices you make for your business. As an entrepreneur, there are a few reasons why you will need to make an item to offer that is, indeed, ready to furnish you with an in excess of one time installment. It is the most ideal approach to capitalize on your item without advertising to new clients constantly. In any case, an extraordinary item will work. You do need to guarantee that the item has advantage that clients need to have.

For what reason would it be a good idea for you to set up a membership item like these through Clickbank? Think about the accompanying:

You can make a common income stream. As such, when you set up this item, you take every necessary step one time and the item continues offering itself, furnishing you with a consistent wage stream.

There are no extra expenses related with setting up an administration like this through Clickbank. Truth be told, you don't need to deal with the installment preparing yourself. Clickbank will take the necessary steps for you, without charging you month to month expenses or some other extra charges from a customary item set up.

There is no important combination between the Clickbank reoccurring installments. As it were, there is no product to introduce on your site. The procedure cooperates effectively and without a blemish.

The framework is set up so as to decrease the quantity of approval decays that happen. In a few circumstances, installments will bomb, for example, if the client has deficient assets in their record. Notwithstanding, the strategies that Clickbank uses to support installments diminish the occasions you will encounter decreases in the installments.

The installments are ensured to you. As such, when you begin being paid through your clients, you can depend on getting your installment frame Clickbank. The organization does not miss making installments.

At long last, when you utilize Clickbank membership administrations, you additionally get the chance to see reports and examination of the action happening over a period. This implies you can see where your weakest connections are and enhance the circumstance.

For the individuals who need a constant flow of salary, don't simply make various installments. You additionally need to structure your items to be pay generators utilizing this kind of membership benefit. It is simpler to do as such than you might suspect!

How Does Clickbank Pay You?

With regards to being a member advertiser, one of the greatest concerns is being paid. There are numerous approaches to fill in as a member. You could contact organizations yourself and set up a relationship that way. You could utilize a portion of alternate administrations online that associate members with item makers. Or on the other hand, you can work with Clickbank. One of the greatest favorable circumstances to going this course is you can truly expand the item deals you get and you can do as such without agonizing over the hidden regular issue. That issue is getting paid.

There are a few things to remember when utilizing Clickbank for your associate deals.

One of the decent things that Clickbank does is to consolidate the majority of your payments. For instance, if you are advancing five computerized items, the organization does not make you keep every one of these different. It joined them, which makes it simpler for most members to gather installment and to know where they are profiting, or not.

Second, Clickbank does all the diligent work. They gather the installment. They process the installments. You don't need to stress over sitting tight for a supplier to pay you. You additionally don't need to handle conveyance of the advanced item. Furthermore, Clickbank handles the exchange without hazard to you.

Another advantage that Clickbank offers that numerous different organizations don't is a more adaptable installment plan. They don't pay each exchange, but they do pay week after week. They additionally have an extraordinary reputation for setting aside a few minutes installments to their associates and their merchants. You can likewise choose to have the installments made through direct store, if you might want to.

Getting paid through Clickbank is simple enough. Truth be told, usually simpler than advancing the items that you need to do. Be that as it may, similar to any administration, it is dependent upon you to keep great records to guarantee that you generally have the best capacity to know where your business stands.

Notwithstanding the majority of this, Clickbank likewise gives you the way to track installments and deals. This can assist you with seeing what is working for your business or if the items you are advancing are what the customer needs and anticipates. Numerous organizations find that these examination apparatuses

are truly how they can maneuver a normal business into a remarkable one.

Instructions to Research Your Niche for Clickbank

As you think about posting an item on Clickbank, you do need to remember that not all items will have a similar value point as the following. The value you can set on your Clickbank item is totally up to you. In any case, it is further bolstering your advantage that you locate the correct cost to set your item at on the grounds that you will probably offer more at that cost. If your item is excessively modest, you are losing cash and you are probably not going to have the capacity to offer a ton of item (individuals may trust the material is contemptible.) On the other hand, if your value the item too high, and can't justify the higher value, nobody will purchase your item. This is likewise prone to drive away associates from marketing your item since it might be valued well out of what others would put resources into.

Things being what they are, how would you know what the correct cost is? A decent place to begin is with some essential research on your specialty, or the region in which you will contend. A specialty is a losing characterized term that essentially implies the gathering of things that your item is in direct rivalry with. It is your specialized topic. It might flame broil or maybe it is beautifying. Whatever the specialty is, that is the place to search for data on the most proficient method to value your item.

The best place to look into your specialty if you intend to list is on Clickbank is at the Clickbank Commercial center, where all items are recorded that are on Clickbank. This is likewise the best place to figure out how to set your associate costs. Search for items on comparative themes as the one you are giving. Look at them by:

The one of a kind data that is incorporated

The length and profundity of the data

The free offers or additional administrations gave

It is additionally a smart thought to discover how well your items will stand out from the rest here. What does your item offer that the others don't? That will be an essential factor here. When valuing your Clickbank item, for all intents and purposes all the data you require is accessible at the Clickbank Marketplace. You have to know the typical scope of valuing for items like yours regarding a matter like yours. Along these lines, you can get a thought of what the market will pay.

How Much Clickbank Commission Can You Earn?

When it comes to making money as an affiliate through Clickbank, the biggest question is this. How much money can you make using Clickbank? The funds made through this service are commission based. Just like selling furniture or cars, the number of products you sell determines how much money you will make. This also means that if you do not sell the product at all, you do not make any money. For that reason, there is no guaranteed income with Clickbank. However, if you select the right product, promote it properly and do your homework, you can make a large amount of money from this service.

One thing that Clickbank provides to the affiliate is the ability to earn substantial percentages of commission. This is not like being a real estate agents and getting three percent of the sale price. Rather, you can earn commissions up to 75 percent. That is much higher than most other affiliate networks on the web, too. In short, the commission offered through Clickbank seems to be higher than what can be made anywhere else. So, why use any other service?

However, you do have to keep in mind that not every product is going to provide you with that 75% commission return. The product creator is able to set the commission rate for their product. Clickbank has a good history of having creators who list the commission at a higher rate, unlike other websites out there. This means that you get to choose from some of the best products to make money with.

The product creator and vendor set the amount of commission you earn. This does not mean that you are limited, though. For example, if you want to help promote a product having to do with Internet marketing, you can scan through the Clickbank Marketplace until you find the product that you want to sell, with the commission you want to earn. Then, decide to promote that one.

As you can see, there is a lot of flexibility here for you, too. It is understood that Clickbank products are some of the best and there is no doubt that with thousands of products to choose from that you will find the product that works for your needs, both in terms of commission and topic. Do check out the 75 percent commission at Clickbank and find out if this is something right for you.

How To Set Up An Affiliate Account With Clickbank

Once you decide to work with Clickbank, the good news is that the process of setting up and managing your account is easy to do. The company has designed itself to be one of the easiest to use affiliate programs today. This means that you have the ability to get your affiliate business up and running quickly. Most businesses can successfully start within a matter of hours, not days or weeks. That means that you can start making money faster than you may have thought.

The first step in the process is to set up an account. To do this, you do not need to pay anything. Rather, you simply need to visit the company's website, fill out the information requested and set up a log in. There is a form, which needs to be completed, but these are

basic forms. If you live in the United States, you may have to pay taxes. The forms are available on the website to set up tax information so that even this process is as easy as possible.

You will need to select your payment options. You can have the company send you a check, but this can be expensive since there is a fee associated with doing so. A better option may be to allow the company to directly deposit funds into your checking or savings account. This is a safe process.

Once you do this, you can then start exploring the Clickbank website. You will find a lot of information available to you to learn and the company really makes it simple to get started. You do not need to know a lot of complex html or other coding to set up your affiliate account with Clickbank. The company will do the work for you.

Becoming an affiliate with Clickbank is an easy process. It does take some work for you to set up and manage your own promotions as you choose to do so, but keep in mind that being an affiliate does mean doing some work. You will find that there are numerous ways to promote your products, but that the job that Clickbank does is very helpful throughout the process. If you have questions or concerns when setting up your account, you can easily get this information through the company. They provide a customer support number or email that you can use if you do end up with a question.

Why Clickbank Can Help You Create A Second Income

Clickbank is a website that connects people. It connects, specifically, those who create products to sell with those who want to help promote those products and earn a commission for doing so. You may not want to dabble in the process of creating your own product, or at least not yet. However, you want to make money at home. You can do this through the resources that Clickbank provides to you. Many people find that Clickbank is the easiest and fastest way to get that second income going online.

How It Works

If you want to promote another's product through Clickbank, your goal is to set up and manage an affiliate service. As an affiliate, you can then sell the products to customers and receive a commission for each of the sales you help make.

By allowing Clickbank into the picture, you guarantee that you will receive payment for anyone who purchases a product through your promotional efforts.

The first step is to sign up for a free account with Clickbank. Then, you will be able to see the huge number of products currently available that you can help promote. The list is big and impressive! Choose something that interests you. Then, you can start to promote it after you have created an personalized link. This link is your ticket to getting paid. Any time that someone clicks on that link, goes to the website and buys the product, you earn a commission for the sale. It is that easy.

It may sound too easy. The fact is, you do have to earn your commission. Your commission has a basis on how many people you get to buy the product, so you do have to do the marketing work and promoting work yourself. This is not difficult to do when Clickbank offers numerous products and tools to help you through the process. Many people find it to be easy to get started.

Why should you use Clickbank for a service like this? In short, you could go out and find others to form an affiliation with, but that will take relying on the other person to tell you what happens within your business. If that is not likely to help you, chances are good that you are going to lose some money here. With Clickbank, you can track your sales right away and you do not have to worry about if the other person will pay you.

Selling Multiple Products Through Clickbank

After creating an initial product to sell through Clickbank, the second step is to create more. As soon as you see just how easy the process is, you can really set yourself up to sell numerous products through your account. You can also use this ability to test different versions of the same product, experiment with different price points and add new products to your line up. The good news is that Clickbank really does give you a large number of options. You have the ability to add up to 500 different products to your account. This includes different versions of the same product.

Keep in mind that to do this, you will need to log into your preexisting Clickbank account and set up the product under your my Products Section. Once this occurs, you will need to save a HopLink Target URL within your account, assuming that you want affiliates to promote your product for you. This will allow you to have one URL per account. This URL is the page that your affiliate traffic is pushed to, where the sale is made and people buy your product. It is usually the same as your Pitch Page URL.

Selling multiple products with Clickbank is a good idea, however you do want to know what you are doing first. If you have one product up on Clickbank, consider the following tips before you set up new products.

Are you getting the most out of your Clickbank product as it stands? If not, is the price wrong?

Do more research on the product, industry or niche. Learn what is lacking in the industry thus far. In other words, what could you do differently to attract new people?

How will you market this product? Is it an add-on to another product you have sold?

Perhaps it is a new product, new topic and therefore an all-new approach is necessary.

The more information you have about the market for your product, the better off you will be. Once you get your foot in the door with the first product you are selling on Clickbank, the rest of the products you hope to sell will be easy to get listed and promoting, especially if your first product did well. Affiliates will want to be in on your new product right from the start if they think it will be profitable to them to do so.

Chapter 2

Incredible Traffic Wave

Making cash online may sound basic in principle, but by and by you require more than the cut---and---dried directions. In online business, activity volume is the key.

At the end of the day, more guests parallels more cash. Expanding the activity to your site can enhance your money inflow by a few means, the most immediate of which is the expanded potential number of offers, regardless of whether by direct installment or commission.

In any case, we are not here to examine the advantages of expanded viewership. Rather, we are here to discuss how to increment said viewership. How might you enhance your site's movement stream?

There are bunches of tips and traps to accomplish this.

Web journals

Initially expected to resemble online journals or methods for individual articulation, today writes are utilized by advertisers all over the place.

As the fame of sites developed, so did the nature of the regular blog engineering, and so today writes have a particularly different look from full---blown sites. As an advertiser, making utilization of online journals is the essential methods for making progress.

Set up a blog utilizing WordPress.

It makes things such a great amount of less demanding, in addition to there is an abundance of modules that can make movement age a breeze.

WordPress is generally a suite of programming segments that make it simple to distribute and deal with a blog. What makes WordPress such an extraordinary instrument is, to the point that you have the alternative of introducing modules – little bits of code that can accomplish a wide assortment of impacts.

There are even modules that perform activities like distributing posts naturally. ShareThis and AddThis are two modules that can enable your guests to impart your stuff to their companions rapidly and advantageously.

Truth be told, you will most likely need assistance while picking the privilege modules, as there are such a large number of decisions, and not all are of equivalent quality.

Post sections consistently to keep things intriguing and new.

Keeping a blog alive and intriguing is constantly harder than beginning it up. Bunches of individuals start up close to home sites with a solitary idea in their psyches, and when they put it down to words, nothing else turns out, and the blog bites the dust a sputtering demise.

Marketing web journals are helpless against a similar ailment. If you need to keep your marketing blog alive and profiting for you, at that point you should post sections consistently. About once multi day is perfect, however once every 3 or 5 days is alright as well.

More posts additionally considers more Internet action, which web crawler insects will get, and consequently concede you enhanced item rankings.

Remain on point.

If you begin getting unimportant, your perusers will get uninvolved. In normal discussion, point changes are normal, and pretty much anticipated.

On non---personal writes nonetheless, things are different. Individuals anticipate that you will remain on point, and anything you put on your blog must have something to do with your item or administration (beside cross advancements – more on this later).

No less than 95% of your substance ought to be identified with your item or administration to some significant level of pertinence. Finding and getting ready substance under such unbending limitations is a test in itself, henceforth the difficulty of keeping a blog alive.

If you need to go off---topic in your posts, make beyond any doubt to put a disclaimer.

Or on the other hand make it conceivable to skip it (if part of a more drawn out post).

Going off theme isn't constantly avoidable, particularly if it can help demonstrate your case.

In any case, while doing as such, one needs to do it in a way that makes it feasible for perusers to get around them, if they are keen on just the meat and potatoes of your blog.

If a whole blog entry is for the most part off---topic, at that point check it with a disclaimer or a label like "additional" or "off---topic" for less demanding perusing and separating.

While going on a sudden digression in a more drawn out post, either make it totally conceivable to skip, or coordinate it so well into the composition that it progresses toward becoming not a digression, but rather a fundamental component. All things considered, if it is an essential contention to support you, at that point it isn't generally off---topic in any case.

Site FEATURES

Sites are pretty much free---form, or, in other words is similarly as simple to treat it terribly as it is to do it right. As an advertiser hoping to enhance his or her site movement, there are things that you can do and things that you can abstain from doing with the end goal to enhance not simply the stream of activity to your site, but enhance the nature of the site all in all.

Make a press page that basically endeavors to motivate guests to present their e---mail addresses. Press pages are not especially new, but rather they are successful. As the general Internet populace moves toward becoming more vigilant against wholesale fraud or even simply spamming, they have turn into significantly less eager to give away their e---mail addresses.

These days, you have to ask it from them courteously and specifically – consequently the requirement for a clear press page. Make it as clear as could be allowed. Try not to put things like "get a free something only to give us your e---mail address", or, in other words. Simply request the e---mail address, no more and no less.

Try not to put video or other substantial components on your crush page

Abstain from diverting the client shape the job needing to be done. The human eye is prepared to spot development, or, in other words precursors made due amid chases or while being chased.

If for instance you put a video on your press page (or more terrible, an auto---played video), at that point you hazard diverting the client and shielding them from topping off the inquiry fields on your crush page.

Keep in mind that the press page is expected to draw out contact data, not to push or offer the item or administration; guests get all that could possibly be needed of that from alternate pages.

Additionally, these overwhelming components can back off stacking and can be irritating.

Give your guests the choice of telling their companions as they finish their information exchange or similarly as they are taking off.

It appears to be basic enough, but it can without much of a stretch net you more e---mail addresses for your rundowns.

At the point when individuals extremely like what you have or if they think somebody they know may like it, at that point enabling them to impart to their companions enables you to famously make the most of current opportunities.

Simply recall that the e---mail addresses you arrive in such a state ought not be mishandled, since they were not given by the proprietors themselves.

Include leave pop---ups with "extraordinary offers" or "possibly you'd lean toward" kinds of messages.

These are extraordinary for publicizing your lesser---known items or then again benefits, or for cross advancements.

Numerous more quick witted Internet clients know how to square popups like these, but the vast greater part still peruses the Internet with least security controls, so there isn't excessively to stress over.

Abstain from putting popups inside the substance pages of the site, as this might irritate clients.

Recordings

At the point when YouTube became showbiz royalty, the Internet encountered a change in perspective. This isn't difficult to understand, as video has a tactile effect that other media don't have.

Some contend that the "communicate yourself" reasoning of YouTube has pushed the improvement of the Web 2.0, where client information and criticism are utilized as substance all by themselves. To nothing unexpected, the ubiquity of video has expanded extraordinarily from that point forward, and today recordings are typical.

Advertisers can utilize these recordings to create movement, but the standard of control applies.

Connection or insert recordings in your posts, as this can energize movement for both your site and your video site profile.

While crush pages are not appropriate for recordings and other overwhelming Web components, your site's landing page is.

In any case, there is as yet a characteristic farthest point of what's in great style and what isn't. Abstain from running over the edge with gaudy impacts and different contrivances. Posts are more appropriate for in excess of one video, but ensure none of them auto---plays.

Obviously, if the recordings you post on your blog are under your name in the video have, you get sees there as well.

Attempt Vimeo.

It resembles YouTube but less standard and not seen as being brimming with futile recordings, as

YouTube once in a while is.

YouTube has a notoriety for being loaded up with senseless, dumb, and generally asinine recordings, in spite of being brimming with valuable stuff also. Vimeo contains a portion of the equivalent negligible recordings, but it doesn't experience the ill effects of a similar terrible rep.

Moreover, having your recordings facilitated on a site other than the big enchilada can mean better buffering for watchers, as the client base is littler.

Viddler is another video facilitating administration that you can experiment with.

On a similar line of thinking, having recordings facilitated on Viddler can be profitable. Viddler is additionally a noteworthy video facilitating administration, so they have dependable administration and sensible buffering speeds.

Make A Video Response.

When somebody makes an inquiry that you need to reply, take a stab at making a video reaction, or, in other words than a straightforward content answer.

A video reaction takes more exertion than the conventional content answer, but what you lose in exertion you gain in client appreciation.

They will feel a more grounded association with you since you "identify" with them and will require the push to accomplish something significant like this.

Moreover, if you are honored with great looks, this is an incredible method to put that common attraction to great utilize. If you are uncertain of how you will perform on camera, audit your accounts and observe what's wrong and right them.

Take open talking exercises if you require them.

Post Videos to Several Websites.

Presenting recordings on a few sites at any given moment is simple if you can locate the correct programming. Presenting on one site is simple, while presenting on 2 or 3 is no biggie.

Anything past the 3---site check get tedious and squanders your time.

Programming like Traffic Geyser can enable you to get use from the mechanization that the PC gives. Movement Geyser likewise works for something other than video.

Obviously, you can hope to pay for such programming, as the makers are as a rule individual businesspeople and advertisers.

Complimentary gifts

What's superior to a decent item or administration? A decent item or administration that is for nothing out of pocket. This has been a typical theory for a very long time.

The savvy representative can make utilization of complimentary gifts to profit in a roundabout way. It might cut into your benefits, but if you make benefit generally, at that point all's great.

During a time of advanced items, free items are anything but difficult to give away, since making duplicates involves two or three ticks.

Individuals love getting free stuff, so every so often set up a type of challenge or giveaway.

Consider it the result of free enterprise considering, but individuals consequently liven up upon the notice of free stuff.

Sadly, it is the result of current private enterprise, specifically marketing, that has made individuals likewise be careful about things that sound pipe dream.

Individuals have a tendency to be suspicious of businesspeople acting so charitably, and we can't generally censure them for it.

Keep in mind that giving without end stuff is cool, but giving ceaselessly excessively looks suspicious.

Add free additional items to buys to knock up the apparent esteem.

One extraordinary approach to build the apparent estimation of your items or administrations is to incorporate additional items. Rebates off consequent buys are decent, but nothing beats a free high---quality item.

A similar guideline of suspicious giveaways applies here. Also, this is an opportunity to move a portion of your less dynamic stock. For advanced items, giving endlessly complimentary gifts with buys is significantly less demanding and more adaptable.

The better the apparent estimation of your items or administrations, the more likely clients are to return and enlighten their companions regarding you.

Huge giveaways are more compelling than little, customary giveaways, so plan your giveaway plan likewise.

With regards to giveaways, the standard is greater is better. All things considered, you will need to plan bigger but less continuous giveaways, instead of littler normal reward days.

Despite the fact that normal giveaways enhance the dependability of money and activity stream, they don't establish as enduring connections as the enormous bashes do.

Timing your giveaways to harmonize with occasions is a smart thought, as individuals are typically substantially more ready to spend then – utilize your complimentary gifts to lure them to purchase the well done.

TAG-TEAM

Where one will fail, the joined endeavors of many can. Collaborating with different advertisers opens up various conceivable outcomes for marketing, notwithstanding enabling the gathering to pool assets for more noteworthy impact.

Try to discover individual advertisers whom you can trust. The essential rule here is to ensure all gatherings satisfy their commitments.

Work with Other Marketers.

Working with different advertisers can help all concerned parties help their activity. Specifying one another's items or administrations in posts is a decent method to support cross---site movement.

This might be somewhat dubious if you are marketing different kinds of items, and it can likewise be cumbersome if you are immediate contenders. Be that as it may, you can work this out.

Connection to Other Websites.

Connection to other advertisers' sites and have them interface back to you under an area like "Our Partners" or "More Cool Stuff At".

Beside less perpetual connections as they show up in posts and passages, you can energize all the more long---term associations and cross advancements by including each other's URLs under a changeless sidebar or menu area.

That way, clients will probably recognize the cross---site joins and additionally see a more extended --term connection between your two sites – which can be deciphered as a sign of trust.

Advance Your Partner's Goods or Services. At the point when a client makes a buy, embed an offer for an accomplice's merchandise or administrations after the request affirmation, and have your accomplice do likewise for you.

This is a simple method to influence commissions and additionally to enhance activity en route. After affirming a request, divert guests to a page with proposals, or create a popup with a similar purpose.

You get paid for what you sold, and open up the likelihood of making some additional off of a commission – does the expression "two feathered creatures" sound well-known?

Offer free stuff from accomplices and they can do likewise for you. Giving ceaselessly

tests and free things all alone can be compelling, but not as successful as having other individuals do it for you.

Enabling your accomplices to distribute something you gave them uninhibitedly enhances your movement since it urges purchasers to look for the wellspring of the complimentary gift.

Support Events.

If you can get enough individuals, you can begin supporting occasions or open substances like nearby bands and sports groups.

One extraordinary thing about cooperating with different advertisers is that it enables you to pool assets. Supporting nearby clubs, groups, and bands is an extraordinary method to make some genuine --world exposure, and part up the expenses between numerous individuals makes it not so much excruciating but rather more fiscally practical.

Email for Your Partners

When you send normal e---mails to clients, you can incorporate offers for your accomplices' stuff as well. As a functioning advertiser, you most likely send e---mails to your supporters on a standard or even unpredictable premise.

These e---mails are ideal for acquainting your accomplices with the supporters. Regardless of whether you connect to them inline or by means of an "accomplices" segment, or even through a footer segment, you can enhance movement for your accomplices, and ideally they will do likewise for you.

Take an interest in Traffic Exchange

A movement trade is where you can get individuals to visit your site if you visit theirs – fantastic for the beginning advertiser. With regards to enhancing activity volume straightforwardly, you can bring matters into your very own hands, or if nothing else your pointer.

Through activity trades you can "exchange" your visits for visits from different advertisers. In addition, this is additionally an opportunity to meet individuals with comparable interests in either movement age or business matters.

Long range interpersonal communication SITES

Long range interpersonal communication is tied in with making associations with individuals and staying aware of what they share with you – and the other way around. As an advertiser, you can utilize a long range informal communication profile as a way to keep associated individuals up---to---date on what's hot and new business--- insightful.

Sign---up for records on sites like Facebook and MySpace, at that point set up a profile for your business.

Numerous long range interpersonal communication locales offer a different class of profile for business clients and big names, when contrasted with normal individuals. These unique profiles get more highlights, but as a rule at an expense.

Be that as it may, utilizing these profiles gives you more opportunity to post heaps of substance, and is inside the terms of utilization. Contrast this with representatives utilizing individual pages as smaller than usual shops, who in the end get found and compelled to close.

Make sure to begin your business right, and adhere to the principles.

While trawling for "companions" or "devotees" to welcome, endeavor to search for the ones who have interests connected to what you bring to the table. Whatever wording your long range informal communication benefit utilizes for associated individuals, it gives careful consideration to what individuals like and detest.

A straightforward look on their profile pages may turn up some helpful data. Concerning profiles with open posts, you can likewise gather something from perusing them. All things considered however, this can be time---consuming and tiring, but there is dependably the possibility of finding the perfect individuals.

If you can pack an association with individuals compelling inside their groups of friends, at that point they can welcome their companions to interface with you. These are the correct individuals that we were discussing – the general population who have solid suppositions and can impact their different contacts to swing to a similar assessment.

It's fundamentally similar to getting proposals by means of the common word---of--- mouth implies. The more persuasive a man is inside his or her groups of friends, the likelier they are to pull other individuals to interface with you.

Utilize MicroBlogging Services

Utilizing microblogging administrations like Twitter and Plurk can make it simple to refresh devotees with brisk bits of news or helpful data.

Speedy and compact is the name of the session of these lightweight interpersonal organizations, but they can be fantastically helpful. If you need to share something rapidly and effectively, at that point make utilization of microblogging. You'll need to figure out how to utilize URL shortening administrations, as these microblogging administrations have exceptionally restricted post sizes.

Utilize Ning or SocialGO

Ning.com is a simple --to---use stage that is incredible for setting up long range interpersonal communication profiles. SocialGO is like Ning, and is amazingly, one more elective social organizing site.

Finding these elective long range interpersonal communication administrations can be helpful as it might enable you to take advantage of specific markets. In opposition to appearances, not every person is on Facebook, and there are a few networks that adhere to these less---mainstream administrations.

The mark "concealed gold mines" is able here.

Utilize Business Social Networking Sites Business---inclined long range informal communication locales like LinkedIn and Plaxo are extraordinary for discovering business contacts and business. building systems all the more straightforwardly situated towards

In spite of the fact that these sites have a tendency to be drier and rather more constrained in substance and client base, they are explicitly made with the end goal of business and in this way the individuals who join self---qualify. Basically, if you are a part here, you are keen on making business associations, regardless of whether as a representative, manager, accomplice, buyer, or dealer.

Composing

While you might be amazed by illustrations and enhancements on contemporary sites, but when it comes directly down to the line, the duplicate makes the site beneficial. Composing duplicate is an underestimated aptitude in many circles, and great marketing specialists are far and few in the middle.

Great duplicate on your site or blog

passages is basic, since awful duplicate is likely to push potential clients away.

Not every person is a language structure policeman, but rather that does not mean they won't be occupied by awful spelling and dreadful sentence structure.

Unbalanced expressing is very different from something that is simply off-base. Whatever dialect you use for your site, do endeavor to make your spelling and sentence structure impeccable.

Compose helpful, useful articles

These should identified with your offered merchandise or administrations and add them to article indexes. This is called article marketing.

The thought is to show yourself as a text style of valuable data, and conceivably quality items also. If suitable, add connects to the substance driving back to your site. Ensure that the article catalog benefit permits this.

Contract A Writer

If you are bad at keeping in touch with, you can contract somebody to do it for you – loads of journalists can be discovered on the web, and some are great while as yet being moderate.

Obviously, loads of individuals have a dread of composing for open review, and this can hamper abilities advancement.

If you would preferably not invest energy constraining yourself to show signs of improvement, procure somebody already's identity.

Utilize Programs that can Post Articles for You

There are PC programs that enable you to post articles to a few indexes at once, so you can get more reach without more exertion.

Presenting on a half---dozen or more sites is repetitive, so why not get programs that can do this for you? The underlying setup is most likely the hardest piece of utilizing these projects, and after that it's everything only a couple of snaps and taps.

Visitor Post

Visitor composing, or composing for another person's site under your own personality, is a decent method to get a few cross---website activity, particularly if the site you are composing for arrangements in comparable things with yours.

This is an extraordinary method to get use off of another site's ubiquity. Obviously, the stuff you compose must be of magnificent quality.

A seriously --written section posted on a prevalent site is certainly not how you win fans. Alternately, you can have somebody celebrated compose for your site, or you can direct a meeting with them and post the transcript.

Web based ADVERTISING

Web based promoting is the bread and butter of web based marketing, so this area will make sure to enable you to out. Keep in mind that the majority of these administrations have a few contending organizations offering them, so glancing around and looking at the best costs.

Obviously, one can't surrender nature of administration for a shabby bill.

Make utilization of pay---per---click (PPC) advertisements

You get the word out while paying for those that as a matter of fact navigate. Pay---per---click is a cost---effective method for motivating individuals to visit your site.

Your advertisements are spread wide, and you are charged for each interesting client who navigates to your site, and not for just having the promotions showed.

Cost---per---action (CPA) publicizing is additionally a feasible decision, and it is more adaptable than PPC.

Cost---per---action is much more cost---effective than PPC on the grounds that you can set it to pat out when a guest accomplishes something more valuable than just visiting –, for example, rounding out a frame or finishing your press page. The rate per finished activity is typically higher than that for one of a kind guests.

Flag promotions may appear to be old---fashioned, but they are as yet found all over the place, so attempt them out.

Less cost---effective but less demanding to deal with, these are as yet the standard charge for online advertisers all over the place. Different web based publicizing organizations offer different sizes and targets, so glance around and pick the ones you feel are ideal.

Publicize on Ezines.

These are normal or semi---regular distributions with directed crowds that may agree with your business interests.

For sure, if the e---zine's intended interest group individuals are, by rationale, adjusted to your offers, at that point this can give you a noteworthy lift in high---quality movement. In any case, know that your rivals may experiment with this strategy as well.

Publicizing on advanced classified advertisements sites can help as well.

The group deteriorates here, but you never know who will come walking around these sites, so posting your promotions here is anything but a terrible thought. Also, these have a tendency to be very shoddy.

Online radio is picking up notoriety, so promoting on these Internet---based radio stations is a smart thought.

Publicizing on these computerized radio stations implies spending a significant aggregate of cash, but it is dynamic promoting that audience members can't skirt past.

Rundown developer sites have bunches of e---mail addresses, so you can take a few and add to your rundown for promoting mail.

For advertisers hoping to work through e---mail, these are veritable crowds of fortune. As a rule these sites contain the e--- mail locations of individuals who have communicated their enthusiasm for advertised items, but there is dependably a possibility that you seem to be a spammer.

Google's AdSense is a setting --sensitive publicizing framework that can convey your advertisements all the more exactly to the opportune individuals.

AdSense observes the meta---data and "depiction" of a website page's substance to set up promotions that have some importance.

For instance, if a site page is for a diversion concerning ships and planes, at that point the promotions that show up might be for model war vessels, or a historical center display about biplanes, or even a flying school. This change in accordance with settings implies better essential watcher intrigue and in this way more viable promoting.

Present your site to online site indexes. It will enhance your general nearness, while tapping into the specific disregarded groups of onlookers.

Beside sitting tight for web search tool creepy crawlies to visit and guide your site out, you can make a functioning stride and present your site URL to site indexes. A few people, especially those searching for sites like one another, will swing to these indexes.

ONLINE INTERACTION

Expanding movement isn't just about inspiring individuals to travel every which way, but additionally making them remain and share. Profoundly dynamic sites get bunches of movement coming in, as well as large amounts of client action on those sites.

Keep in mind that the action level of your site likewise factors into your web crawler positioning, so getting this up is exceptionally prescribed.

Join Forums

Join gatherings, or set up your very own and make your contributions by associating frequently with individuals, rather than lording over them with your authoritative forces.

If it is your discussion, use your forces dependably. All the more imperatively, effectively take part in discussions that intrigue you or have something to do with your business. If you claim the discussions, at that point taking an interest like this enables the individuals to feel that you are not kidding about tuning in and associating with them, and the regular human reaction is to acknowledge and welcome this.

Utilize an Auto---Responder

Setting up an auto---responder appropriately can help decrease outstanding task at hand while enhancing client benefit and fulfillment, in addition to you can embed interfaces as well.

Auto---responders are fairly dubious things, so you will require a considerable measure of tweaking to make them work right. When you do in any case, you will discover your remaining task at hand enormously facilitated.

Give Quality to Traffic Coming from Social Bookmarking Sites.

You can utilize social bookmarking destinations like Digg, Reddit, and StumpleUpon to use fame from clients, but you need to ensure that your site is high caliber, or else you will get set apart down.

Keep in mind that the intensity of social judgment can cut both ways. This can be eccentric since you can never be very certain how the group will take it. More awful, individuals tend to make utilization of the principal individual's response as a reason for examination, which means your initial couple of introductory impressions will do much towards driving the group towards or against your support.

Remark and offer your thoughts

Try to be significant and abstain from including excessively promoting stuff to your remarks or gathering marks.

Include your remarks and voice your sentiments, but dependably make certain that you are on indistinguishable wavelength from every other person. Embed joins when fitting, and ensure that your discussion marks contain at least promoting substance. Keep in mind that you tread a barely recognizable difference among "spammer" and "client with some promoting goals".

Answer inquiries on Yahoo! Answers, and when helpful, notice your site. Hurray! Answers is a network that enables individuals to make inquiries and find solutions from the network.

Be useful and fair, and attempt to give answers that are really valuable. There are additionally other such sites, some of the time with specific settings, but the general thought is to search for inquiries that are inside your capacity to reply, and slip in an advertisement when the circumstance permits it.

Composing an ordinary bulletin for sending out to endorsers is an extraordinary method to keep them on the up and up and you in their psyches. These pamphlets are normally sent into e---mail inboxes, but having a duplicate on your site is a smart thought since it gives new guests a thought of what they can get, and likewise fills in as a reinforcement for your customary guests and clients.

IRL ADVERTISING

Because you maintain an Internet business, for what reason would it be a good idea for you to constrain yourself to Internet---compatible media for publicizing? In---real---life (IRL) publicizing methods can work as well. While different organizations request that IRL watchers visit their block --and---mortar areas, you will request that they visit your location in digital

Promote in Newspapers

An ever increasing number of organizations are promoting in daily paper classified promotions and guiding perusers to their site – you can do likewise. It bodes well in light of the fact that a URL (especially an abbreviated URL) makes it simple to fit loads of data into a little physical space.

Obviously, other offering duplicate will be required nearby the URL, but for the full points of interest invested individuals can visit the page made reference to.

Print notices and post them on open announcement sheets or different spots, as long as you have authorization to do as such.

These can be sheets in network lobbies or even the nearby staple goods and general stores. You can even post in coffeehouses, if the supervisors permit it.

You can even incorporate tricks like tear---off tickets with codes on them for extraordinary rebates and so on. Plan flyers and hand them out to individuals with a grin, or slip them under auto wiper cutting edges and the like.

Get out there and get some daylight and exercise while advancing your business. Similar standards apply for flyers – nothing excessively showy, or guarantees that are "unrealistic".

It is dependent upon you how extravagant you need to make your flyers, but you will dependably require the correct state of mind to make the collectors truly look and analyze what you just gave them.

If you see somebody perusing your blurb, you could stroll up to them and converse with them about it.

This can be very viable at changing over watchers into clients, but it takes a ton of guts and some fortunes as well.

Individuals are somewhat suspicious of aggregate outsiders who stroll up to them and need to talk, so you should present yourself and your business first. If they won't tune in, nimbly enable them to take off. A large portion of all, be considerate, amenable, and appealling.

Business cards make presentations and confront --to---face publicizing simple.

When meeting potential business gets in touch with, it pays to have business cards arranged, as they can make sharing contact data as basic as anyone might imagine. Furthermore, it fills in as an update each time it is seen, though a uninterested individual will dispose of your discussion very quickly.

Utilize word---of---mouth promoting.

Converse with your loved ones about what you're doing, and they can tell their different colleagues. Tell them what you're up to and inquire as to whether they have room schedule-wise or are intrigued.

You can either request that them straightforwardly advise their companions or abandon them to do it all alone.

Utilize Radio Advertising.

In spite of the fact that radio is winding up less and less prominent, radio promoting is as yet a suitable methods for publicizing your site, products, or administrations.

Radio is as yet a free wellspring of stimulation, and it keeps on being normal, so why not make utilization of it? Loads of radio stations offer sensible rates for promoting on air.

Physical mail is another decision.

Regardless of whether you do it through the postal administration or drop post---card type promotions in individuals' letter drops. You can likewise distribute flyers and handouts in said post boxes.

These can be effortlessly discarded as garbage mail, but that is the reason you have to work with expansive volumes of these messages, to build the odds that somebody will really open it up and read through it.

Either that, or discover some approach to make the letter truly stand out but not hazardously. Setting something massive and harmless inside can work.

Exploit Street Level Advertising Street---level promoting, for example, putting stickers or publications on your auto, is a strange and consideration -- snatching approach to get the message out. As a matter of fact it may make you resemble an instrument, but if it works at that point it's justified, despite all the trouble.

Official statements

Official statements are not only for celebs and huge --time organizations. Indeed, even private ventures can make utilization of public statements. Declare your open opening, new items or administrations, and so on. You will require great composition and flawless planning and the correct spots to distribute.

Public statements are extremely valuable if you know instructions to compose and distribute them.

A public statement has a different vibe from general instructive or limited time material. This is the reason official statements can be difficult to pull off, particularly if you are set in a publicity -- pushing advertiser attitude. In these cases, if you are not sure, get some gifted help.

The tone of public statements ought not plan to offer, but to illuminate. This is with the goal that individuals won't quickly believe it's just an offering strategy, and accordingly enhance the volume of guests supported by public statements.

This is a kind of delicate offer, where one enables the peruser to think of a game-plan as opposed to prescribing one. This likewise for the most part enhances the nature of guests, as the individuals who do drop by are frequently more intrigued than the easygoing bystanders.

Spare official statements for significant occasions.

This incorporates a redid site, another item or benefit, or for declarations for enormous occasions that you will hold.

A public statement is a noteworthy declaration, so don't mishandle it. A VIP does not make a public statement for a walk---on job in a film, but a lead job will positively warrant one.

In like manner you may not deliver official statements for ordinary giveaways, but the occasion bashes unquestionably might be justified, despite all the trouble. Use your official statements reasonably and you will think that its giving you pleasant blasts of movement.

Deals

Beside offering from your site, there are different approaches to offer them as well. Truth be told, offering it in different ways makes it significantly more available to different individuals, and in this manner enhances your business straightforwardly and activity in a roundabout way. To urge them to visit your genuine site, offer a markdown by means of a connection in your item depiction.

Offer on eBay.

Offering on eBay is a smart thought since it makes offering items simple while enabling you to take advantage of a gigantic market. The model of installment depends using a loan cards, so you ought to have some method for tolerating installments.

Ideally, your ledger ought to be appropriate for tolerating numerous installments over brief timeframes, which implies that it ought to be a business account and not an individual record. Make sure to pick the correct class for your item, in light of the fact that eBay bargains in pretty much everything, so you have to ensure invested individuals can discover what you bring to the table.

Offer on Amazon.

Amazon.com, as eBay, is a decent place to offer stuff, but just if your item is a book, a white paper, or a sound book. Amazon centers around the scholarly class of items, so while its extension is more restricted, its client base is more focused on.

Self---help books in computerized design are extremely famous here, so you can make some significant benefits by means of Amazon. Also, there are a few chances to profit as an afterthought through Amazon Associates, so set aside some opportunity to look at that.

Exploit the Kindle Fever.

If you do have books and other protracted content items, think about distributing them in Kindle organize, since the great as well.

Fuel is getting great buzz. Different configurations as are PDF

What you ought not discharge are specifically editable archive groups – like MS Word reports, RTF and TXT documents, and so on. The Kindle design is especially pleasant in light of the fact that the Kindle gadget is intended for advanced perusing anyplace, which makes it an ideal stage for most online advertiser scholarly items.

Blended BAG

This segment contains those tips that don't exactly fit in alternate segments, but will absolutely demonstrate fascinating and worth experimenting with. Utilize them as they seem to be, or consolidate them with different strategies for synergistic outcomes.

Set up your blog or site with RSS, so your endorsers can get your posts as they go on the web.

A few people have something many refer to as "information compulsion" – these are the individuals who get anxious if just the same old thing new comes up on their feeds each hardly any minutes, or the individuals who monitor their profile pages time after time. Exploit this, or just keep clients refreshed as the news thinks of RSS. RSS is anything but difficult to set up and use; truth be told, it does essentially everything naturally after the underlying setup and tweaking.

Utilize Audio Instead of Video.

Utilizing sound rather than video can make your site less demanding to stack, and will diminish the quantity of individuals who leave in light of the fact that your page won't stack rapidly. This is a simple trap that can truly enhance the nature of your site's client encounter.

The truth of the matter is that sound records are substantially littler than video documents. In addition, the nature of sound records is less demanding to modify, as human ears are not exactly as touchy to changes in "quality" as the eyes seem to be. What number of individuals do you know care for sound quality more than or even on indistinguishable level from designs? Regardless, the speedier your page stacks, the snappier the media is cushioned, and the more nonstop and stammer --free the experience is.

Be Nice

Being decent and considerate is essentially great practice all around, but applying it online can enable you to abstain from losing clients because of impoliteness on your part. This is really self-evident, but for reasons unknown individuals tend to change their identities on the web. May be it is the expulsion of the immediate association that makes them feel they can be less limited.

Notwithstanding, as a representative and by and large decent online individual, it is to your greatest advantage to dependably be considerate and courteous. You can pull in a larger number of ants with nectar than vinegar, as the well-known adage goes. It likewise gives your depreciators and rivals less ammo to use against you, notwithstanding enhancing the nature of your associations with your clients, who may even talk up for your sake in instances of contention.

Get Your Ads Seen on Book Inserts.

Book embeds are basically little sheets with notices embedded into books, which enormous --time merchants like Amazon do, so search for how to get your promotions on these supplements. This is a neglected territory of low---level publicizing. It very well may be exceptionally successful in light of the fact that the getting parties are keen on the item it is incorporated with.

This intrigue rubs off on the promotion embed, all the more so if the advertisement is firmly identified with the item. Practically speaking, this is improved the situation physical books, but it should likewise be possible with different items, and even with computerized items. For instance, one can incorporate an advertisement for a flame broiling cookbook with another grill barbecue, or a promotion for a book of sew designs with each obtained weaving manual.

Apply SEO.

Apply SEO to your site and presents on improve creepy crawly results from web crawlers, and increment your significance and hunt rankings. Website design enhancement, if you have not known about it, is "Site improvement", an arrangement of systems utilized via web crawlers to refine the nature of ordering and along these lines deliver more important outcomes each time a hunt is asked.

Obviously, advertisers can change their material to expand the impact of this. As an advertiser, your assignment of applying SEO systems implies improving your site look and more pertinent for your given specialty. This involves utilizing the correct watchwords, setting the privilege meta---data for website pages, and more.

Web optimization is an expansive and profound subject, and there isn't sufficient space to talk about it here, so you are in an ideal situation finding a book or course managing only on the topic.

Purchase terminated space movement and get guests who are diverted from sites that never again exist.

Activity from guests searching for sites that have terminated by and large goes to squander – they wind up being diverted to pages offering to offer them the spaces. Why not get the activity diverted to your site page? As a matter of fact it may not be at all identified with your business, but rather a strategy is a legitimate strategy if it works, and this absolutely boosts your movement figures.

Chapter 3

Affiliate Marketing Super Shot

Partner marketing is an outstanding method to begin profiting on the web, since you don't need to contribute much (or any) cash, you don't must have your own items, and you don't need to manage client administration or transportation.

All you truly should be effective in associate marketing is a powerful urge to succeed and the learning to get it going. I can't give you the inspiration you require, but I can positively kick you off with the learning you require.

In this report, you will take in the essentials of beginning with partner marketing. You'll figure out how to pick gainful specialties, how to pick the correct offshoot items to advance, and how to get activity to your offers.

All that I will encourage you will require practically no forthright speculation, and almost no specialized information. These are extremely fundamental methods that totally anybody can learn!

So we should begin...

The primary thing you have to do is pick a specialty to advance. This isn't as simple as it sounds. You can't simply pick a specialty - you should pick a beneficial specialty. Few out of every odd specialty will be as gainful as you may trust.

I have picked specialties in the past that I genuinely anticipated that would be beneficial, yet in spite of my earnest attempts I was not able locate a solitary subsidiary item that would change over all around ok to endeavor worth the time included.

Luckily, I have figured out how to decrease my odds of picking failure specialties. Only a couple of straightforward advances can enable you to take out a portion of the danger of picking these unrewarding specialties.

Conceptualizing

Your initial step is to make a rundown of specialties you're occupied with advancing. Simply make a not insignificant rundown of specialties you think may be beneficial, or that you're simply intrigued by advancing.

Try not to stress over something besides making a rundown of 10-20 specialties at this moment. If you require enable, you to can simply check out you for motivation.

Check out your home. Things like kitchen machines, open air grill hardware, office supplies, varying media gear, and melodic instruments are generally specialties you may spot around your home.

Peruse a book shop – either on the web or disconnected. Attempt Amazon.com or a book shop in your nearby neighborhood. Peruse the books or magazines.

Investigate news sites for interesting issues. Check destinations like Google Buzz for new patterns.

Checking Potential Profitability

When you have a rundown of 10-20 specialty thoughts, it's a great opportunity to begin narrowing them around looking at their potential productivity.

There are three fundamental ways I do this:

1. I verify whether there are any magazines being distributed in the specialty. This is once in a while, but not generally a pointer that a specialty may be gainful.

2. I verify what number of individuals are promoting on Google AdWords for the specialty. Individuals aren't probably going to promote as once huge mob in a specialty that isn't productive, particularly if the CPC is high.

3. I check the MSN Commercial Intention device for the absolute most mainstream business sites in the specialty.

I extremely like the Commercial Intention device. It's really exact. Suppose I need to be a partner for golf gear. I would enter something like "golf clubs" in the instrument, select the "Inquiry" radio button, and then snap "Go".

For the expression "golf clubs", the business expectation is 0.97, or, in other words impeccable 1.0. This implies the specialty is certanily gainful, as by far most of individuals who scan for that expression will likely be occupied with purchasing.

All that you do in partner marketing will require catchphrases. Regardless of whether you utilize PPC marketing, article marketing, blogging, or some other type of marketing, you should pick the correct catchphrases if you hope to get a not too bad measure of movement.

I utilize the Google Keyword Tool for brisk and free research:

https://adwords.google.com/select/KeywordToolExt ernal

This catchphrase apparatus is amazingly simple to utilize. You just enter your seed watchword expression and you will get an expansive number of related catchphrases. You can sort them by the normal number of month to month seeks.

You need to search for catchphrase expresses that have:
1. Somewhere around 1,000 month to month seeks
2. Less than 50,000 contending destinations

To check rivalry, you need to enter every catchphrase expression in statements into Google. This will reveal to you what number of individuals are focusing on that correct expression.

When you have a rundown of watchwords that have somewhere around 1,000 month to month seeks and less than 50,000 contending pages, it's an ideal opportunity to utilize those catchphrases to get activity.

There are truly hundreds, maybe thousands of approaches to get activity, but I'm simply experiencing probably the least demanding approaches to get movement rapidly and with next to zero cash in advance.

Article Marketing

One of the most effortless approaches to get free activity is by composing articles and submitting them to article registries. Many article registries have great expert with the web search tools, so articles you submit will regularly rank well rapidly and acquire activity.

If you will send individuals straight to an associate connection, it's a smart thought to enlist a space that you can use to divert individuals to. There are several purposes behind this.

1. You can undoubtedly change the member connect if fundamental, without returning and alter huge amounts of articles.

2. Some article registries require it.

Articles ought to be somewhere in the range of 300 and 500 words. It's really a smart thought to keep articles genuinely short so you don't exhaust individuals, and in light of the fact that you don't need them to feel totally fulfilled. To get the great data, they have to visit the associate connection in your asset box toward the finish of your article.

Some article catalogs to submit to include:

http://www.ezinearticles.com

http://www.buzzle.com

http://www.goarticles.com

http://www.articlesbase.com

http://www.articlecity.com

Blogging

Blogging is another extraordinary method to get activity. It's ideal if you do it all alone area with your very own facilitating, but you can likewise make utilization of free blogging stages like Blogger.com if you need. Simply know that they have the privilege to erase your blog whenever, for any reason they pick, regardless of whether you didn't disrupt any guidelines.

Each time you make a blog entry, make certain to incorporate catchphrases in the title of the post, and additionally the substance. This will help guarantee you get a lot of movement from the web search tools.

Social Content

Social substance destinations like Squidoo.com and HubPages.com have great expert with the web search tools, so the pages you make will regularly rank great.

They are free, and are additionally greatly simple to utilize, regardless of whether you don't have any specialized understanding. You don't have to know HTML, in light of the fact that their online wizards will enable you to set up pages in a matter of moments.

Similarly as with blogging or article marketing, you should make sure to utilize your watchwords in your titles and substance. This is the best way to guarantee you'll get movement from the web crawlers.

Discussion Marketing

Discussions can be incredible for partner marketing, but you must be watchful. Most gatherings don't enable you to post offshoot connects in posts or in your mark, so read the standards painstakingly. You may have the capacity to connection to your blog from your mark if member joins aren't permitted.

Presently you have the nuts and bolts you have to begin with member marketing. You can take this data and keep running with it, and you can be profiting very quickly!

Whatever you do, you have to keep at it. Never surrender! Trust me, these things truly do work. Member marketing is to a great degree simple, and once you make them moneymaking strategies set up, they can run for the most part on autopilot!

Join these techniques with your very own portion and you'll have a relentless cash machine that just continues turning out the money for quite a while.

Chapter 4

The Most Brilliant Marketing Strategies

1. An Introduction

It's hard for us online advertisers to go anyplace when we put inquiries to our universities just to be given a wordy, perplexing and difficult to understand reply.

It's additionally hard for us online advertisers to give the responses to probably the greatest inquiries on our universities lips when the appropriate responses themselves are not straight forward at all.

The two sides breed irritation and dissatisfaction. That is the reason we've assembled the main 15 addresses that we get asked the frequently, and addressed them in the most straight up, non messing around way imaginable, everything from asset working to give a strong procuring establishment to your organizations, to getting guests and creating the most deals and benefit from them, to specific reasons that some succeed and some don't.

2. Goals Of This Section

- To go straight for the throat and answer the most habitually made inquiries by online advertisers and to tackle these issues appropriate here and at the present time with the goal that you never need to ask them again.

- To set out the central issue of 'How would I get hits to my site?' and answer it in the most straight forward way.

- To set down central issue number two 'How would I fabricate my rundown?' and answer you in the most straight forward way.

- To solidify and install the idea of asset building and how they snowball and manufacture themselves in your psyche, the main key to progress.

- To set down central issue number three 'I've purchased X measure of aides previously and they didn't work for me. For what reason is this one different?' and to reply in the most straight forward way.

- To set down central issue number four. 'How would I get my offshoots to really advance something, they don't appear to ever make any deals' and obviously, to reply in the most straight forward way.

- To talk through every one of the above inquiries in a discourse organization to bolt tight every one of the ways out with the goal that you can rapidly, effortlessly and altogether understand the response to every single one of them.

Welcome, and welcome to the best fifteen fast fire question and answers segment. All through this territory we will take fifteen of the most well known inquiries asked by online advertisers, place them in a rundown, and answer them in the snappiest conceivable way. The reason I needed to get this in here, is on the grounds that much of the time, it's not uncommon to see individuals who haven't achieved their objectives identifying with online business, going from manual for guide, posting in discussions making these extremely broad inquiries. As a general rule, they're either overlooked, individuals endeavor to offer them stuff guaranteeing this to be the huge answer they've been searching for, or the appropriate responses they get are simply not straight sufficiently forward and go off on digressions, don't give the full story or even veer off from the first inquiry through and through.

I recollect when I previously began, I was soliciting a considerable measure from inquiries, picking up as much understanding from anybody I could discover. The disappointing thing was not exclusively did I once in a while find a solution of any substance that I could follow up on, but I can see now that half of it was add up to waffle in any case. It was relatively similar to no one really knew the responses to what I was inquiring. And in this way, I present you with the main fifteen speedy fire Q&A area, which will expel every one of the disappointments of not finding straight solutions about, what are in my eyes, a blend of the best fifteen needs of advertisers, combined with what appear to be the most asked and slightest best addressed inquiries.

I trust this will make things a considerable measure clearer for you.

3.   Question 1: How would I get hits?

This must be the main inquiry by online advertisers, and I run over it routinely, and all things considered. After all without getting hits to your site you can't offer anything. The issue isn't just do the vast majority approach this the wrong way, but when this inquiry is drawn closer either straightforwardly or through aides, they're giving inaccurate answers as well, which, if you've asked it previously, will comprise of getting a type of administration or some kind of advertisement that will take care of the majority of your movement issues. In spite of the fact that this may appear the best approach at first look it's very counter gainful to your endeavors.

One thing I need to indicate out you initially is that your underlying point isn't to get hits to your site by any stretch of the imagination, and getting a monstrous measure of them isn't a need. Understand that you just need to pull ten or twenty thousand hits altogether, ever, to your destinations to make them fruitful. Obviously this will go up as you advance through your asset building, and that is key here. The assets that are assembled and that you can use again and again. (That is your huge 5, associates, list, clients, long haul clients and joint endeavor accomplices).

The issue comes when somebody instructs you to go out and purchase advertisements from wherever it may be, web search tools, e-zines, whatever. If you don't have the asset accumulation strategies set up to gather the huge 5, you will must start from the very beginning again with your advancement each and every time you dispatch an item. This is the correct reason that, regardless of what number of hits a few advertisers get to their destinations, they will never procure in excess of a few thousand dollars multi month benefit, if that even.

The second issue comes when individuals expect, or are surely told, that you have to get a huge number of hits to be a win. This is unquestionably not genuine either, albeit again I perceive how it might appear that at first glance. That is the reason I generally show introduction items and follow-up extensive items, since let's be honest, what number of $1200 items do you have to offer in multi month to rise to your present individual pay from your activity, if you have one, or to achieve your objectives of having all the more available time, more cash in the bank and so forth.

Additionally, lets not dismiss why we began in web based marketing in any case. It unquestionably wasn't to spend monstrous measures of money attempting to get your site details to peruse high numbers. Numbers don't mean quality, regardless of what anybody lets you know, this is actuality. Look at one single 10k rundown of joint daring to 100k supporters of an e-zine advertisement. I guarantee you, for a begin, you'll get more snap throughs from the JV in any case but set up the numbers together and you'll get a far higher level of offers through the single quality joint endeavor.

So how would you get more hits to your site? Well leading the inquiry is void since all the more once in a while implies you'll show signs of improvement results. Search for quality, and the appropriate response is joint wandering, constructing these assets, and having others advance your items for extremely high commissions to pull in the numbers. If you're just hitting a couple of thousand hits for each month from these joint endeavors, that is not an issue. Disregard ensured hits, overlook e-zine advertisements for straightforwardly advancing your site and overlook web crawler situating. They may acquire you increasingly the method for numbers, but it's huge deals we need, not huge numbers. In that circumstance dependably think quality over amount, or, in other words entire of this report is instructing.

So ask me again when you've done two or three joint endeavors and have started to fabricate your subsidiaries, your client base, your contacts and your rundown, how would you get hits to your site? That is the reason you've been building your assets. That is the place your visits and deals originate from. The more items you dispatch, the more assets you assemble, the less demanding this is. The most costly tedious part is beginning. After this current, it's modest, brisk and simple to reuse what you've accumulated to create an endless stream of visits and deals.

4. Question 2: How would I assemble my rundown?

One more of the most every now and again made inquiries, in the web based marketing scene, that comes particularly from individuals who haven't made their own items yet is how would I fabricate my rundown. Everybody has gotten a handle on the idea of building your own media outlet, that you can elevate to over and over without paying a penny, that generally comprises of the most focused on individuals, and the individuals who will purchase your items on the grounds of trust and the nature of your past work.

And that in that spot is the way to everything. When you have your very own rundown that stretches over the five thousand check, you ought to at any rate have one item, and the larger part of individuals ought to have originated from the advancement of that item. Abstain from anything that approaches you for money to put endorsers on your rundown, in light of the fact that, if you haven't attempted them as of now, let me guarantee you that contrasted with what you can accomplish through joint endeavors and different means, the nature of the rundown will endure in spite of the fact that not really it's size. As we discussed above notwithstanding, the quality issues for both your present advancement and your future advancement.

Estimate is certainly not everything here.

The manners by which we're constructing your rundown don't include coordinate strategies. Something that you can connect cash to, get up toward the beginning of the day and abruptly have a monstrous responsive rundown to elevate to. Concurred you may wind up with an enormous rundown but they'll be a long way from responsive.

Focus your endeavors on advancing your items and in the meantime, whatever move somebody makes through your locales, ensure that they wind up on one of your rundowns. If we take a gander at things along these lines, everything necessary is for them to either purchase something, information exchange for something, hop into some development, join your associate program and so on.

Never make anything that enables clients to experience the business procedure on your site, or any procedure whatsoever so far as that is concerned, and then lose contact with them. This isn't the best approach to get things done. Obviously, speed is likewise an issue for some, individuals out there. I'm certain you would prefer not to stay nearby just to locate a couple of years after the fact that your rundown has just achieved a few thousand endorsers. You need a great deal, you need a major rundown and you need it rapidly. I understand how it is and I abhor sitting tight for things to develop after some time as well. This is actually why we ensure that all that you do, identified with your site, includes gathering names and email addresses for your rundown sooner or later.

How about we take a gander at a few numbers beginning off with the straightforward joint endeavors. Say for instance you score a joint endeavor that brings both of you thousand visits from somebody's close to home rundown. Presently with standard e-zines I can understand how you probably won't consider this to be by and large much, as the quantity of individuals who buy in, contrasted with the quantity of individuals that visit,

can to be sure be lower than you anticipate. But through joint endeavors, with these quality records, I've seen membership rates top one out of three, and it's not surprising for no less than 25% of your guests to buy in to something if your business duplicate is doing it's activity.

That may not appear to be a great deal at the present time, but rather suppose you take ten joint endeavors and figure out how to pull in a rundown of 5k, which shouldn't be excessively of an issue if the nature of your JV's is decent and high and you get a decent number of visits. A 5k list is all extraordinary, and you'll likewise be profiting through deals on those joint endeavors. Despite the fact that when you begin to couple in your member bonuses that you ensure are genuine high, actually, so high that you may not be making an immediate benefit, the assets will cruise in.

This is your benefit. Not the cash from the deals, but rather the assets that you're building. This is the reason you surrendered $50 per deal, and it's your subsidiaries combined with joint endeavors that are going to, if you'll pardon the buzzword, set your rundown expanding ablaze, numbers savvy as well as speed astute. Each and every time you discharge another item, you will add an ever increasing number of individuals to your rundowns that you can elevate to and have advance for you. It's another snowball impact, or, in other words this implies you know the more you put in, the more you will get out, and each and every item that you discharge will build your assets, your rundown estimate included, and will add to your advancement control for future items. Consequently you'll make an entire load more money than you would have done by different means and techniques.

Before we proceed onward I need to ensure that you understand how this functions. Individuals make their own rundown building locales that are outfitted straightforwardly to building their rundowns. This is incredible, it works, but when guides reveal to you that you should focus every one of your endeavors on building your rundown, it sort of makes me somewhat furious now and again, for the basic reason that they're not giving you the entire story by a long shot. It's alright to take a gander at rundown working as one of your principle needs, and to be sure it ought to be, alongside building members, clients, long haul clients and joint endeavor prospects, but for it to be fruitful, you need to incorporate it into your other marketing strategies, and this is the thing that most neglect to let you know.

Once you've aced this and understand, once more, how every one of these assets tie into one another, and can't be viewed as independent substances, you'll see greater and better outcomes, and they will come all the more rapidly as well. Presently if you consider what I've recently let you know, and venture back, you ought to have the capacity to see promptly how this isn't an instance of go out and get as greater rundown as could be expected under the circumstances, as fast as could reasonably be expected, all alone. This is the thing that numerous aides educate, but similarly as with the accomplishment of the entire framework it's integrating assets in through the dispatch of your own items.

5. Question 3: I've purchased X measure of aides previously, for what reason didn't they work?

Amazing, great this is a central issue. While we don't profess to be immaculate inside and out to all individuals, there's everything way of things that I've seen amiss with different aides, but I don't care to harp on it, I'd preferably converse with you

regarding why these manuals are different, and to the extent I'm concerned they unquestionably are.

I had a thought quite a while prior that was identified with every one of the things I wish I knew before I began, and at different phases of my web based marketing profession. I chose that when I made sense of this entire thing, I would compose the greatest and most splendid guide and utilize each snippet of data I have in my mind that I've learned throughout the years identifying with how to end up fruitful in web based marketing, and here we are, you're understanding it.

What I've attempted to do, and ideally prevailing over this and the other 14 manuals, is toward the beginning of each report, give you clear objectives with the goal that you know precisely what you're realizing and for what reason you're realizing it. Likewise toward the finish of the reports we have outline segments that show you precisely what you've figured out how to do. What I would not like to occur, was to get this out available, and have individuals come to me and say that they don't picked up anything by any stretch of the imagination. This was the purpose behind this specific style of introduction.

The manner by which this differs to different reports, is it connects every one of the holes however many routes as could be expected under the circumstances. For instance, what number of different reports have you perused that reveal to you how to accomplish something but not why? How might you adjust and learn if you don't know for what reason you're accomplishing something? Or then again perhaps they disclose to you why you ought to accomplish something but not let you know precisely how to do it. Perhaps they even disclose to you the how's and whys but it doesn't function and this reveals to me that, there is a missing bit of the riddle some place and, they haven't revealed to you the full story.

So what makes what you're perusing right now different from the others? Well the reality I haven't forgotten anything here, and you have my pledge on that. There are no insider facts that I don't need you to know and there's not a measure of cash or achievement that I don't need you to have. Truth be told, when you get propelling your own fruitful items and have some overwhelming assets all alone, I trust especially to have the capacity to joint endeavor with you, and catch wind of your examples of overcoming adversity, and obviously for you to tell other individuals.

With this very guide, while some will state it's excessively dubious on the grounds that it doesn't disclose to them well ordered, to click here, go here, purchase this, advance, others, which I'm trusting will be the lion's share of perusers, will state hello, better believe it, I've filled in the holes now and I have a feeling that I'm sufficiently sure to go out and advance my own items that I make. Get my own contacts, my very own rundown and stand alone two feet. If something changes now you know why and, the points of interest of precisely how everything functions and ties into different parts of this entire framework, it enables you to change and adjust the manner in which you work together without anyone else terms.

This is the reason I trust that you will end up in a hell of significantly better condition in a years time than if you were to purchase another well ordered taking you by the hand digital book that just points of interest one information, and one result. This is for what reason you will succeed utilizing the new information you procure here, where others have flopped, essentially on the grounds that you were just already given an exceptionally shallow take a gander at the universe of marketing, and have been informed that there is just a single most ideal way. Presently you know different and can cut your very own way utilizing the layouts given in each area all through this specific course.

6. Question 4: How would I get my associates to really advance?

An intriguing inquiry, possibly not as vigorously asked as a few, on the grounds that numerous advertisers out there haven't really got to this stage yet, despite the fact that it's one of the principal issues you will run over once you begin maneuvering members into your framework.

Back regarding the matter, so how would you get associates to really advance for you? Well the main stage is drawing in them in any case. Obviously, without offshoots they're not going to advance for you. This is a major piece of your introduction item and the motivation behind why you should set your bonuses decent and high (55% up to 90%), particularly when you're beginning. You can't bear to pass up subsidiaries information exchanges as a result of the gigantic advancement potential they hold.

Presently after you've pulled in them in any case, you're probably going to discover the huge issue of why the hell aren't they advancing my stuff for me? All things considered, there are a couple of purposes behind this. One of them may really repudiate the inquiry, and the response generally is, they are advancing for you they're simply not doing it successfully. As I'm certain you've made sense of as of now, the quantity of individuals that know how to advance associate projects and have their own assets that enable them to do as such, for almost no expense, is far lower than the individuals who have presumably never discharged their very own items and, subsequently, don't have the rundowns and the ability to advance viably.

There are a couple of courses around this, but I ought to caution you ahead of time, if you figure out how to get yourself a hundred partners joined, don't be stunned if just four or five of them make any significant measure of offers. Beyond any doubt you'll get others that possibly make a low number of offers, but high volume requires experienced advertisers with assets that have just been developed. So don't be put off, don't be concerned or believe you're accomplishing something incorrectly if you're partners aren't performing. It's in all probability that they don't know how to perform.

The genuine offshoots that you will see and that will be making you a considerable measure of cash, are the ones with the enormous and successful records with great reaction rates, which I need to state are rare. This doesn't really imply that none of your offshoots will make any deals, but I need you to get ready for the way that scarcely 10% of them will be experienced.

Hits can't simply be a decent pointer of somebody's advancement control either. For instance, I recollect my first involvement with this. It included me getting up one morning, and investigating my subsidiary details, and seeing that there's one individual in there that is had over a thousand hits come through medium-term, but not a solitary deal.

Presently you can envision how stressed this had me, since when I did my testing I was pulling in one deal each forty to sixty five visits. So normally, being a little jumpy that my direct mail advertisement wasn't up to scratch or something had turned out badly all through the business procedure, I sent him, and his answer put my brain very still. He'd really gone out and purchased a bundle of ensured hits. By this stage the quantity of visits happened to go flying up to the five thousand stamp and still just a single deal for him. I'd been around the houses, and seen a considerable amount of hit programs and so

on, and I realized that it wasn't my business procedure that was to blame, it was his absence of learning identifying with how to advance offshoot programs.

So you see it's not forever your blame. The quantity of guests acquired by the members don't generally think about the nature of your business framework. Saying that, it is in every case best to check your business framework for shortcomings if you begin to see an odd number of guests come through and an absence of offers contrasted with, the examination you did and, your own discoveries through your own techniques for advancement. It can, be that as it may, be your blame totally on occasion. Again this is the point at which your exploration comes in and you need to attempt and make sense of what turns your partners on. Do they require uncommon offers or something to that affect? Or on the other hand are they unpracticed and ailing in information about how to advance all in all.

The best way to discover is to test. Send them a couple of offers, a couple of extraordinary arrangements that include higher commissions the more deals they make, or even send them advancement guides and a little information about how to advance for themselves if you fondle to composing such aides. Remember however, if you see weird details, guests to deal proportions, or individuals just getting little measures of visits, it's as a rule, not going to be your blame. Either hit them with offers, instruct them, or continue building and wait for a greater amount of those joint endeavors or individuals with a lot of involvement and enormous records and assets for advancement of their own. Beside that, everything else is down to the individual and their aptitudes, and practically out of your control, so don't be put off if your initial one fifty or so partners never make any deals. You'll get bounty more, again snowballing, the more items that you discharge.

7. Summary

- Greetings and welcome to the main fifteen fast fire question and answers area, where I'll be taking probably the most regularly got some information about internet marketing and noting them. These appear to be simply the most prominent inquiries, and others, are asked, and things that I woefully needed to know right off the bat in my profession but nobody appeared to have a straight forward response for me. A disappointing knowledge, something we'll squash at the present time.

- Let's begin with inquiry one. How would I get hits to my site? Effortlessly the main inquiry by online advertisers on the grounds that, just, no hits implies no deals. Something that most go about in the wrong way, or have been instructed erroneously on such huge numbers of events, they feel tipsy from the conflicting data they've been given. So we should answer this inquiry unequivocally in two sections.

- Part one is to change the inquiry. The point of web based marketing isn't just about getting hits to your webpage by any means, and getting a gigantic measure of them isn't a need either. Ten or twenty thousands hits can without much of a stretch mean $40,000 in addition to worth of offers for an exceptional item. So how would you get hit's to your site? Well you don't. How would I get quality focused on hits to my site? This is our new inquiry tending to the more pertinent inquiry.

- Resource building is the key. It's tied in with pulling in assets that you can use again and again. Never giving a solitary contact or client a chance to circumvent, staying in touch and making normal arrangements over different items through JVs.

- The most costly and hardest piece of web based marketing is getting clients at first, and the issue comes when somebody instructs you to go out and purchase advertisements from wherever it may be, web indexes, e-zines, (which you definitely know isn't vital). If you don't have a few asset gathering strategies set up. You will must start from the very beginning again with your advancement each and every time you dispatch an item. This is the correct reason that regardless of what number of hits a few advertisers get to their destinations, they will never gain in excess of a few thousand dollars multi month benefit, if that even.

- Problem two comes when individuals expect or are informed that you have to get a huge number of hits to be a win. Not genuine, this is the reason we have introduction items and follow-up items, to battle this issue of low transformation rates from individuals who don't know or trust you yet. The common stream of free, to shabby to costly deals with this issue for you, along these lines reusing assets you've effectively gathered without the additional cost of beginning once more.

- Look for quality not amount, and the appropriate response lies in joint wandering or PPC web indexes (Which is an entire other book in itself.), assembling these assets, and having others advance your items for you. If you're just hitting a couple of thousand hits for every month from these joint endeavors, that is not an issue, if you're pulling in those assets. In addition to the fact that they are quality, will give long haul benefit and dependability for your business. Disregard ensured hits and overlook e-zine advertisements for straightforwardly advancing your site. They may get your increasingly the method for numbers, but it is huge deals we need, not huge numbers. In that circumstance dependably think quality over amount, or, in other words entire of this report is instructing.

- Question Two. How would I assemble my rundown? One more of the most much of the time made inquiries in web based marketing, in light of the fact that everybody believes it's the most important thing in the world of their prosperity, which it isn't the point at which you factor in the intensity of building JV contacts, associates and rehash custom.

- The most ideal approach to assemble your rundown is to dispatch your very own items full stop. To start with, abstain from anything that offers to put endorsers on your rundown for cash. They're either paid to land on your rundown, age old or different sold supporters that cause you harm with your host or ISP, phony, disgraceful quality and just not worth your time not to mention your cash.

- The manner by which we're doing this doesn't include any immediate rundown building strategies, as with all our different assets, it's much an instance of dispatch your item, get the underlying couple of joint endeavors out and ensure that you have all your asset building devices set up and pull them in. You're not substituting deals for assets, or assets for deals, everything occurs on the double, and gets greater, and greater, and snowballs again and again, the more items you dispatch.

- There's no mystery it truly is this straightforward, and this is one of the uncommon situations where an engaged line of reasoning doesn't function and in addition dealing with everything without a moment's delay. There's no real way to isolate these strategies since they're altogether associated. Separate them and the supply of new assets that one supplies to another is broken (associates fabricating your rundown through advancing your item for instance) and you need to fall back on what most of the general population out there are doing to their disservice. Starting from the very beginning again each time they dispatch an item which is both costly and tedious, and not to anybody's greatest advantage regardless of what the business.

- Let's take a gander at a few numbers to back this up, beginning with a basic joint endeavor that conveys two thousand visits to your site from somebody's close to home rundown. Two thousand isn't a considerable measure using any and all means, particularly not spread over numerous JV's, and it is anything but a hard thing to accomplish. With the nature of these rundown composes, as we examined prior, it's not unbelievable for membership rates to add up to 25% of visits if your business duplicate and asset manufacturers are doing their activity.

- This may not appear to be a great deal at the present time, but rather when only ten little joint endeavors makes a rundown of 5k, and who knows what number of associates, future contacts and clients all cooperating. It beyond any doubt includes. When you hit that five thousand stamp you're set in light of the fact that every asset has just begun to manufacture alternate, as long as you never separate these ten joint endeavors for one item, either with new contacts, current contacts, your clients and your associates. Keep in mind that we discussed increase your bonuses to absurd levels on your introduction items? This is the reason. What number of visits would a measly one hundred members, combined with JV's with the best entertainers, bring you? And what number of out of those thousands of visits do we know buy in to records and free stuff? When you have some time begin to work out a few numbers, make them traditionalist, extremely moderate, and watch how utilizing this framework you can without much of a stretch force gigantic measures of advancement power and benefit from the most modest number of assets and rapidly as well.

- Moving onto question three. I've purchased X number of aides as of now, for what reason didn't they work? This is a tremendous inquiry, and the general population that ask this frequently don't understand that an entire book could be composed regarding why different aides didn't work for them. This is the reason it's such a hard inquiry to answer straightforwardly to the disappointment of the individual asking and the individual attempting to reply.

- I had a brainwave back when I began. I just couldn't make sense of why I wasn't being a win. I said to myself 'When I turn into a win I will compose a book, or a guide, noting every one of these inquiries that I can't discover answers to and ensure the perusers have the appropriate responses that I don't'. This was the first historically speaking thought in my ideas organizer. Six or after seven years, you're understanding one of those extremely manuals.

- I trust that numerous reports tumble down for a few reasons in spite of the fact that there is, no ifs ands or buts, some astonishing data out there, alongside the not all that astounding. Most need clear objectives for one. If you don't know where you're going, how would you hope to arrive. It resembles requesting bearings via telephone and getting an answer like 'It's over yonder'. It simply doesn't work.

- The second thing. Synopses. Less demanding to focus on memory by a wide margin. Data is no great if it is difficult to recall. These are for the most part fundamental things that I've seen numerous aides need and something that, I found from my first site, can be the difference between a peruser picking up, understanding, focusing on memory at that point making a move, or tumbling down at any of these stages preventing them from being a win.

- Next. Poor data, but not simply mistaken data, more awful. Ever observed those reports or purchased a guide that says 'Do this, this then this, click here and then do this' and so on? Everybody turns out with a similar business. Without choices and just a set way to pursue, and data that doesn't discuss why things occur, they don't give the peruser the space to adjust after some time to make their very own business and cut their own way.

- Let me ask you something unique. Name one thing that we've just talked about that contributes to the ruin of numerous advertisers and squares them from progress. Anything by any means. Alright currently, disclose to me why that squares them from progress. What's the reason that this factor prevents them from being effective? How might you maintain a strategic distance from this? Do you perceive how you've just picked up something imperative, data about stuff that occurs as well as why it occurs, and by knowing why it occurs, you can make your own inferences about how to settle it. The why question is so imperative but under utilized.

- For this reason, some may state this guide is ambiguous, but observe nearly, in light of the fact that what you're increasing here isn't simply learning, but the capacity to understand the complexities of every strategy. This thusly demonstrates to you generally accepted methods to accomplish something, why it occurs and at last, will display the end to you so that you can adjust it to your business as opposed to simply being a clone of anybody's matter of fact.

- Ok lets proceed onward to address four. How would I get my members to really advance something? Not as intensely asked as some different inquiries, this is valid, but that is on account of many don't know how to get members through introduction items and high commissions in any case. Presently you do, in any case, this inquiry turns out to be exceptionally important.

- The answer is you can't, not generally. There are two circumstances in which I'd like you to be cautious of. The first is the point at which an offshoot has thousands of hits but no deals. This may not really be your direct mail advertisement or your business procedure, but a member without the right assets to advance viably, perhaps spending on ensured hits or something to that impact. The second circumstance is simply the partners not advancing. Try not to worry if just five or 10% of your members ever really get any hits. Again this could be because of absence of assets, the absence of information

or then again the absence of exertion on your subsidiaries' part. It is anything but a weird wonder so don't be stressed when you go over it. It's very typical for myself, and the various advertisers I remember testing about it when I originally got a little stressed in the wake of running over it out of the blue.

- You see it's not forever your blame and the quantity of guests acquired by the associates don't generally consider the nature of your business framework. Nonetheless, saying that, it is in every case best to check your business framework for deficiencies if you begin to see an odd number of guests come through and an absence of offers contrasted with the examination you did and your very own discoveries through your own strategies for advancement. It very well may be your blame completely now and again. Again this is the point at which your exploration comes in and you need to attempt and make sense of what turns your subsidiaries on. Do they require unique offers or something to that affect? Or then again would they say they are unpracticed and ailing in learning about how to advance by and large?

- The best way to discover is to test. Send them a couple of offers, a couple of uncommon arrangements that include higher commissions the more deals they make, or even send them advancement guides and a little information about how to advance for themselves if you fondle to composing such aides. Remember however, if you see abnormal details, guests to deal proportions, or individuals just getting little measures of visits, it's usually, not going to be your blame. Either hit them with offers, teach them, or continue building and wait for a greater amount of those joint endeavors or individuals with a lot of involvement and huge records and assets for advancement of their own. Beside that, everything else is down to the individual and their abilities, and essentially out of your control, so don't be put off if your initial one to fifty or so associates never make any deals. You'll get bounty more, again snowballing, the more items that you discharge.

- That's just for this area. We have another two of these FAQ segments coming up concentrating on progressively imperative inquiries. All there to ensure you get the down and out in the most immediate way that is available. As should be obvious, there are such a significant number of perspectives to each question, that is not generally the most effortless activity. See you in the following area!

8. Goals Of This Section.

- To additionally take a gander at the best as often as possible made inquiries by online advertisers and answer them in the most unpolished, understandable and straight forward way.

- To approach and talk about the responses to the famous inquiry number five, 'I don't have my very own item, what would i be able to offer?'

- To squash all stresses over not prevailing so that your brain is obvious to move advances as opposed to investing your significant time and vitality contemplating stuff that may or probably won't occur.

- To discuss how individuals are making 20k+ every month, and to clarify how this is absolutely achievable given the right conditions.

- To examine joint endeavors encourage in noting the inquiry 'You continue discussing joint endeavors, but I can never appear to score any, what gives?'

- To answer the ever famous inquiry; 'I would prefer not to make my own items, I simply need to offer different people groups stuff through associate projects, how might I approach this?'

- To loosen up you and evacuate the issues of data over-burden coming up to the pivotal advancement stages for your recently made items.

Welcome, welcome to the main fifteen brisk fire FAQ section two, where we'll be replying in the fastest and most direct way that we can, the best inquiries on people groups lips when they consider web based marketing. We secured the best four inquiries in the past report and now we will proceed onward with the following six, so right away, how about we do it.

9. Question 5. I don't have my very own item, what would i be able to offer?

A decent inquiry that surfaces on numerous events, even a large number of my dear companions who see me staying here working ceaselessly at whatever point I sense that it. They frequently ask me, 'How might I begin my very own business?' The reaction comes that you require a thought first for your own item. After a fast contemplating look towards the sky, they turn back and answer, but I don't have my very own items what would i be able to offer?

Indeed, the basic answer is if you don't have your very own item you will experience serious difficulties offering anything, on the web or disconnected. There's so much crude advancement control that accompanies having your very own items. Take a gander at it along these lines, without them, you can't joint endeavor, you can't have a multitude of members advancing for you, you can't control the business procedure and increase new learning through your exploration, you can't develop your assets for future advancement, truth be told, there isn't much good to leave not having your own item.

So make one. The more drawn out time you spend glancing around in your objective market, the less demanding it will be to think of thoughts for your very own item. I don't hope to plant this guide before a random individual who figures everything we do is send messages out throughout the day and trick individuals (which is by all accounts the standard joke when I notice to somebody that I'm in web based marketing) and then instruct them to make an item all of a sudden.

Similarly, if this was truly your first day in the business I wouldn't anticipate that you will have the capacity to go out and make your very own web based marketing item. You need the learning first, regardless of whether you're not making a data item. Once you've wound up blending with the group and getting down and purchasing items and conversing with individuals, it's extremely uncommon that you can leave a circumstance without concocting another thought, level out of the most straightforward of circumstances.

A decent case of this is a discussion I had a long time back with a kindred advertiser. He'd quite recently composed a shed heap of reports and needed to accomplish something somewhat uncommon with them. Lamentably he needed to experience every one physically and do this by hand. We just couldn't discover a bit of programming to do this for him

(Sorry, I can't let you know precisely what it is, on the grounds that it seemed like that would be his next endeavor). But as should be obvious, just by living as an online advertiser, it's genuine simple to concoct item thoughts that are answers for issues you may have.

What about disclosures? I've had these as well, not really with internet marketing, but rather when you're attempting to make sense of how to accomplish something, and after a drawn-out period of time considering, it comes to you, you give it a shot, and it

brings about the ideal result. That is significant data you have there that could undoubtedly be sold. Keep in mind that when you come to making an item, it doesn't need to be a household item or something that costs many dollars to fabricate, it tends to be something as straightforward as data contained inside your head that individuals will need to purchase, or a bit of programming, that additionally by and large has low overheads, as you can pay somebody to finish the assemble and then go off and offer it.

The decisions truly are perpetual, and the more thoughts you concoct, the more thoughts those thoughts will generate. It just takes one plan to make a five or six item adventure that could last you an entire year. Whatever you do however, don't skirt this. Try not to state ah well, I'll simply advance different people groups stuff, since you'll end up similarly situated this time one year from now going about things like that. It's tied in with making items that enable you to manufacture your assets, and beginning not making your own, is not feasible.

10.   Question 6. I'm stressed that I won't succeed, that individuals will state no dislike my work. What do I do?

Proceeding onward now to address number six. If you're stressed that you won't succeed this time, or that individuals won't care for your work, have no dread since you're not the only one, and I trust this is beneficial to a degree. To the extent my experience demonstrates me, there are three sorts of individuals out there. The primary sort are the individuals who don't generally mind. They simply need to

profit so they toss any old thing out there as fast as possible. This is most likely unfortunate, and we can't be doing with awful quality items.

At that point there are compose two, who are without a doubt made a fuss over what individuals need out of an item, what the responses will be and so on. Thus they ensure everything is up to scratch and as well as can be expected make it before it's discharged. To the extent I can tell, the lion's share of good advertisers are at this stage. That doesn't mean any individual who isn't doesn't have the capacity, but it could well mean they're trapped in an endless cycle, and going no place quick, and this is the place things get harming.

Sort three, the advertisers that need everything to go easily, similarly as the above states, but have an issue completing anything in light of the fact that it is possible that, they've flopped previously and have an issue returning from that, or they're stressed what individuals may state to them, which a portion of the time will be things they truly would not like to hear. For instance, a straight up no I'm not inspired by your joint endeavor proposition and on the lighter side of things, and the odd peculiar client that chooses to send injurious sends. (We as a whole have one regardless of how great the item, let me guarantee you, in which case a cool, considerate supportive answer frequently does the activity to settle the circumstance).

What you mustn't do is given your past encounters a chance to stall out stuck, and get all of you worked up about not having the capacity to prevail later on. Everybody commits errors, and you can't please everybody all the time despite the fact that it would be decent. So regardless of what you do with web based marketing, or some other business so far as that is concerned, don't let past

encounters prevent you from advancing. If somebody doesn't care for your stuff, that is fine, insofar as you're alright with it, give them a discount, or simply take it on the nose, say alright at that point and proceed onward.

Try not to let this kind of thing keep you down. I unequivocally trust this is one of the integral reasons such a large number of individuals out there will fail, in light of the fact that in spite of the fact that they might work extend periods of time and placing everything into their business, they're keeping away from the things that they truly need to do as a result of past encounters. Try not to fall into this snare, continue moving and be consistent with what you're doing. Try not to escape it. If what you're doing isn't working, you need to endeavor to take a gander at what you have to do to advance, at that point do it, since when you do, you'll end up with significantly more trade out your pocket, much more extra time on your hands, and a business that is pushing ahead not standing still.

This is an obstacle everybody needs to get over if they will go anyplace in internet marketing.

The thing is I can't do anything from here to change that. It's absolutely in your hands, so know about what you're doing constantly, and ensure you're pushing ahead. Going around in circles or standing still doesn't tally, and if you do end up thumped a little by somebody's response to you work, recollect, it's not all that much, it's simply matter of fact, and hello, you're the simple one to single out, on the grounds that they've never met you. You can wager somebody, some place will take out their disappointments on you since they can't accomplish what they need, and place the fault on the item that truth be told does work, and you can be glad for.

11. Question 7. How are individuals making 20k+ per month? I can't get close to that figure.

That is one hell of an enormous inquiry, but I won't abstain from noting it thus. Rather I will simply ahead and converse with you about the main motivation behind why these online advertisers are out there and making their gigantic month to month entireties of money that most could just dream of gaining in an entire year.

The principal huge piece of this is the assets. What number of individuals out there do you address all the time that reveal to you that they can't pull in enough business to keep them above water, or to profit? Indeed, even that they're befuddled about how the enormous folks can circumvent discussing their gigantic livelihoods when they've purchased every one of the aides, and have this abundance of information that has been passed onto them.

The enormous thing that you'll discover the majority of these individuals are missing is the use and the labor. Next time somebody asks you this (if they never have, they more than likely will do later on when you begin propelling your own items) you ask them what they're doing to advance. E-zines will come the answer, ensured hits, hit trades, lead buys and the like. This isn't the method for the educated online advertiser, they know superior to that.

Lets expect that you've set up the entirety of your deals and following frameworks, and

have propelled your first item or two alongside a partner framework set up, a methods for rundown building, Jving and staying in contact with your clients and long haul clients. What's the difference among you and the precedent above? It's the use. When you complete such a framework and begin putting your sensors out, making contacts and pulling in offshoots, you're likewise carrying with you a hell of a great deal of advancement control regarding the quantity of individuals advancing for you.

Give me a chance to make another inquiry. If I were to reveal to you that you needed to make twenty thousand per month for instance, you have a half year to accomplish that status, but you need to utilize standardized publicizing strategies. No joint endeavors, no partners, no new contacts and so on. How might you do it? More to the point would you need to do it in any case, since when you take a gander at how things ought to be done, it's far less demanding to understand why individuals come up short and keep on falling flat, while those of us who understand this keep on prevailing again and again.

Keep in mind that we spoke already about getting things done without anyone else. This ties into that, and it doesn't take a virtuoso to work out that twenty individuals advancing your item with indistinguishable productivity from you, at 50% commissions, will get you ten times the measure of offers than you would have alone, with ten times less costs for you, also the time it would take for you to attempt and carry out the activity of ten individuals.

When we discuss these things in this guide, we're not skirting the real issue or rehashing a similar thing again and again. We truly are demonstrating to you's what, and how to succeed.

Having a group of offshoots behind you, sponsored by various joint endeavors with their own advancement for a large portion of the benefits is a decent arrangement. When spreading your endeavors like this current it's undeniably likely that you'll succeed in light of the sheer number of individuals advancing for you, and the flow your site gets.

So all that really matters, how are huge advertisers making so much money consistently? The appropriate response is basic. And it's that they have heaps of individuals advancing their items in different routes the greater part of which fundamentally rotate around standard subsidiaries and joint endeavors or they have developed the assets, as a rule through these way to have that sort of advancement control themselves. Take a gander as of now savvy on your part. How long multi day do you function right now on your online business? I'll go for five hours for precedents purpose. It appears to be a decent mid route between the full time advertiser and the part clock.

Presently what amount do you acquire? Suppose once more, for this models purpose, a thousand dollars per month. Alright, now what amount might you want to gain? Let's assume you'd like 30k per month. Do you see that to make that much money at your current level would take you 30kx5 hours in multi day? So at your current level you'd need to work 150 hours every day to achieve that objective, which isn't even conceivable. The measure of individuals you have behind you and advancing as members and joint endeavors is the way to achieving these apparently incomprehensible statures. Use.

Because it's your own business, it doesn't mean you're the special case that will advance it. That my companions, is the manner by which the enormous folks profit, when scientifically, taking a gander at it from a sole dealers perspective, it looks relatively unimaginable. I guarantee you it's definitely not.

Understand this and you'll begin to perceive any reason why, and all the more essentially how, you can apply this to your business.

12.   Question 8. You continue discussing joint endeavors, but I can't score any, what gives?

Joint endeavors is an extremely intriguing subject. Numerous individuals lamentably misunderstand the idea when they're advised to go out and get joint endeavors. If you're experiencing difficulty pulling in the arrangements that you have to get your business off the ground, the principal thing you have to painstakingly take a gander at is who precisely are you reaching about these joint endeavors.

Numerous individuals assume that the response to every one of their issues is to get a promotion to a rundown through the huge names, but with this comes an issue.

Envision you were acquiring somewhere around 20k per month and discharging your very own items, had a pleasant estimated rundown of clients, and a substantial offshoot base, and this is broadly known. Every one of the general population that believe you're the solution to their concern, and the rundown and individuals you're in contact with are the solution to their issues, you can envision what number of joint endeavor ask for sends you will get each week. Every one of these individuals out there that see you procuring such money, and believe that if they gain admittance to your rundown, they'll acquire this money as well.

This isn't the situation by any stretch of the imagination. When we talk about joint endeavors, I'm unquestionably not encouraging you to go out there, choose huge worker from the sack, get in touch with them and attempt to get an advertisement to their rundown, in light of the fact that there are as of now such huge numbers of individuals doing likewise. So except if you have something added to your repertoire in the method for assets and items as of now, it won't be anything but difficult to end up being justified, despite all the trouble. And by the day's end, that is what we're all doing including me.

Each time I contact somebody for a joint endeavor, I'm in a position where I need to pitch myself and my item to them, ended up being worth their while, and you're doing the very same thing. As you can envision, if you have a couple of items added to your repertoire as of now, this will be far simpler to do this, particularly to the huge names.

Try not to stress however, all isn't lost and, there's much more potential out there than you may might suspect. When we already discussed buying in to people groups records as an initial phase in the joint endeavor tasks, we were discussing, the greatest names that you know as well as, the ones where will probably get a reaction and saw, just on the grounds that there aren't such a large number of individuals competing for a similar thing.

This shouldn't imply that you're making due with second best, a long way from it. There have been a lot of locales that I've joined beforehand that showed best partners, those that clearly have the huge focused on assets officially developed to elevate to. All through these names I run over a portion of the huge folks, that is valid, but it may amaze you to discover that no less than ninety five percent of those best associates I've not known about previously. They're not enormous names, but rather they beyond any doubt get as much money as the huge names.

Don't for a minute imagine that your assets are restricted to the ten or so huge folks you know, since let me let you know there are thousands and thousands of individuals out there, even simply taking the web based marketing scene for instance, that are doing extremely well, despite the fact that they haven't accomplished this nearly big name status with your specific hover of advertisers.

Remember this, and don't feel caught or obliged by being tricked into supposing you need to contend with many others for a solitary joint endeavor. This isn't to imply that you shouldn't contact enormous acclaimed names by any stretch of the imagination, or ever, but be prompted, numerous others are doing likewise. One joint endeavor with a moderately obscure can be significantly more ground-breaking than joint endeavors with the outstanding as well. Everything relies upon the assets they have in hand, so if I could give you one tip about joint wandering, and one tip just, it is enlarge your hunt, and don't simply adhere to those that you've found out about.

Gratefully, we're not restricted to one tip, so I will give you another huge one and ideally put your psyche very still. Presently when you make and dispatch your own item, and figure out how to pull your objective number of joint endeavors, don't fuss and stress over how hard it was, on the grounds that, I won't lie, making the contacts in any case is by a long shot the hardest part, but, once more, this snowballs. You meet individual one, who acquaints you with individual two, three and four, and so on keeping the need to go out and search for new joint endeavors for every single item you make. You basically don't need to do it.

What's more don't disregard the general population you've done joint endeavors with

previously. Work with them once more, take a gander at their proposition, tune in to their thoughts and what they need to state, and you'll see that once you have your initial couple of you don't have to go out doing the majority of that once more. Sort of making one major hover of advertisers that advance every others stuff and joint endeavor with one another.

That as well as include the way that after your initial couple of effective items with this framework, for need of a superior word, is set up so that you will assemble your assets, and be quite hot joint endeavor material yourself. Above all, it's at this stage, regardless of whether your name is just known by your clients and offshoots, that they will begin coming to you with proposition which will enable you to build up your as of now rather expansive heap of assets and advancement control.

So you see the extent that joint endeavors are concerned, it's solitary something you need to do vigorously a few times, in light of the fact that after this you will be the one that individuals are seeking out. If you put in the diligent work now, and set up everything as we've said in this report, and fabricate your assets in the meantime, you may not be a tycoon in a half year, but rather you will have a compelling decent base of assets to begin moving towards accomplishing your objectives for your life and for your business. This is the thing that this entire guide depends on, not making a little benefit as fast as could be allowed, but fabricating your assets as fast and as adequately as possible, making your life of advancement a straightforward instance of four messages and a couple of discussions for every item you dispatch. Obviously there's a trick, and that is, if you need that to transpire later, there's a considerable measure of leg work to be done now, or, in other words what numerous individuals need to hear, but I can't lie. The impact I'm truly

endeavoring to place crosswise over in this report is that it doesn't need to be moderate, it doesn't need to be hard, exhausting or costly, but it will require exertion. Trust me when I say, the outcome is justified, despite all the trouble.

13. Question 9. I don't need my very own items I simply need to advance partner programs, but how?

As you may have speculated this inquiry will be fundamentally the same as the past inquiry identifying with what you can offer if you don't have your very own item. My recommendation would be, once more, to make your very own item.

Regardless of whether you don't need one, it's astonishing how much extra advancement control your very own item gives you and every one of the assets it can get. I think what we have to ask here is for what reason don't you need your own item? I can understand how cool it must be to consider having the capacity to simply mail your rundown and rake in the money without doing any extra work, but you're truly undercutting yourself if you go straight for this choice.

There are anyway two cases where it is very. That is it is possible that you've just got yourself a heap of assets and a major rundown to elevate to through past items, or you figure out how to get yourself in at the highest point of a huge program that everybody joins, and you're only that great at 'enrolling' and assembling your down line. If you're not, the most ideal approach to learn is your very own items and you can simply go hard and fast member advancement later when you have assets customized to that need. If you've been informed that it's as simple as diving in a heap of your

money for leads and hits and stuff, overlook all that. It's simply not genuine except if you're intending to spend a large number, which I don't perceive any reason why anybody would, in light of the fact that there are a lot of quicker, more viable approaches to do this, with your very own item. Have I sold you on that yet? The other option is web index marketing, anyway that is an entire course in itself and a very surprising topic by and large.

14. Question 10. I have this data, but where do I begin?

A decent inquiry, truth be told, it's undeniable glancing through this report and the majority of alternate manuals I you approach. We've endeavored to place everything in the best request we can, from where we trust it's least demanding and snappiest to begin for you. Be that as it may, you may have seen that a considerable measure of the areas we've secured as of now connect to past segments from various perspectives. Lamentably this is something that must be done when composing these reports or you'd have everything in copy.

With respect to web based marketing, regardless of where you are in your vocation, the beginning spot is dependably the equivalent. Regardless of if you have a reserve of partners or a major rundown and past clients as of now, in certainty that is extraordinary. Whatever you do, don't feel like you need to dump everything and start from the very beginning once more. This isn't the situation. I would state that all organizations begin with five things. A thought and a craving to build up that thought, the instruments you have to do as such, the planning and foundation to make everything conceivable, a financial plan, and a business opportunity for your item.

Without a thought you're going no place. With a smart thought, then again, you're headed to various items that you can make and offer at different costs that will no uncertainty produce different thoughts. If you need to take things further, you have to keep your mind open, and dependably take a gander at methods for creating and advancing that unique thought into the most ideal shape for the general population who will be getting it and bringing forth more thoughts from your unique arrangement.

Before you begin you're additionally going to require the devices that will shape the premise of your business. Like we made reference to in the making a base for your business report, there truly isn't much out there that you truly should be effective. The main things that you'll truly need to spend for are, an offshoot content or participation, access to following apparatuses, and autoresponders to keep up your rundown. That is extremely next to no contrasted with the acquiring potential that they bring you. In addition, they're each of the erratic buys that you won't need to burn through cash on again and again. This is a quite decent arrangement when you consider in many people groups eyes you have to spend for advancement over that. We currently realize this isn't the situation by any stretch of the imagination. This is additionally applicable to your financial plan, which doesn't need to be colossal.

When those instruments are set up, that is the vast majority of your readiness and foundation done. You should simply opening an item into your business framework each time and off you go.

In conclusion an objective market. Somebody to pitch your items to. Except if you're super brainy and think of an absolutely unique thought, it's reasonable there are different items out there effectively attempting to take care of similar issues for

it's clients. Do some examination to look at the opposition, but don't be overpowered by everything. There's a lot of room for everybody. And hello, rivalry for your brand new thought is something to be thankful for, in light of the fact that this implies there's as of now a business opportunity for your item, and individuals with access to the clients that you should connect with to offer it. This should comfort your mind straight away.

Finally, and above all, wherever you choose to begin, kindly do begin. We're here giving all of you this data but you should accomplish something with it. Ask yourself, over the most recent a half year, how far has my business pushed ahead? At that point ask yourself how far would you like to push ahead in the following a half year. Would you extremely like to continue everything at a similar speed, or might you be able to hunker down and get twofold, triple or even fourfold the measure of work done through dispensing with diversions and concentrating on the arrangement not the issue. That is absolutely in your hands currently, but do begin. Begin today.

15.   Summary

•   Greetings, and welcome to the brisk fire FAQ section two, where we'll be replying in the fastest and most direct way that could be available the absolute most regularly made inquiries by online advertisers as observed by us all through our profession. We've just taken a gander at four inquiries and concoct some prolific answers for them identifying with different segments in this course. How about we proceed and examine the following six inquiries.

•   Question number five. I don't have my very own items, what would i be able to offer? A decent inquiry that is upon numerous people groups' lips, even those in the beginning times of building up their business, some of them haven't chosen they need to begin a business.

- The straightforward response to this inquiry is if you don't have your own items, you will have a substantially harder time being a win on the web or disconnected. It's certainly feasible, simply substantially harder. There's so much you have control of with your own items, from the crude advancement control and the extra assets to, fitting your marketing to the item, and notwithstanding fitting your items to your marketing now and again, things you can't do advancing different people groups stuff.

- If you're having issues thinking of new thoughts, don't stress. It just takes one to be a win, which we know as of now can produce a few at any given moment.

- I wouldn't anticipate that you will have the capacity to think of thoughts instantly either in light of the fact that basically you can't take care of issues identifying with a subject that you don't think about. Therefore the more you blend

with advertisers, their items and your objective market, the more you will learn, understand this and the better you will get.

- A great case of this is a discussion I had with a kindred advertiser half a month back. He'd quite recently composed a mass of substance and needed to sort out it especially, but couldn't locate a robotized procedure or item to complete this activity successfully. A straightforward circumstance and item thought that just introduced itself once engaged with this specific market. Not something you'd select off the highest point of your head.

- So the response to the inquiry 'I don't have my very own item, what would i be able to offer?' is just your own item. I wouldn't suggest going some other way if you're simply beginning a direct result of the power it gives you for future advancement.

- Question Six. I'm concerned I won't succeed, or that individuals won't care for my work. What do I do?

- Similar to the past segment where we discussed a portion of the encounters you may have as an online advertiser, I think this inquiry is in reality truly gainful sometimes when taking a gander at the nature of work completed. Be that as it may, by no means should it prevent you from advancing and pushing ahead with your business.

- There are three sorts of individuals out there. Sort one, they don't especially think about something besides profiting as fast as possible. Undesirable for them and their clients, we can't have disgraceful items skimming around out there.

- Type two, they're fretted over what individuals need out of an item, their responses and so on. Thus they ensure everything is

up to the most elevated standard conceivable before it's discharged in a fast effective way. The lion's share of good advertisers have this outlook, but it's fundamental not to stall out stuck, got up to speed in something for a long time when everything necessary is a couple of long stretches of work to make clients overjoyed.

- Type three is the advertiser who needs everything to go easily but has an issue completing anything since they're drawing on their past encounters excessively. Gaining from them is great, keeping down in light of the fact that you're concerned something terrible may happen again is decimating. This kind of dread should be confronted and hit head on, which can be hard if you're by and by joined to your business the same number of us wind up throughout the years.

- The fundamental principle here is this. If you know in yourself that you've put forth a valiant effort, and the lion's share of clients are content with your endeavors, you know you've worked admirably regardless of what anybody says to you, if you're content with it, and your clients are content with it (beside the odd unavoidable time when you turn into an objective for people groups dissatisfactions) at that point manage it, and proceed onward, and push ahead. This is a major key to progress that no marketing aides appear to convey to the surface for some reason. It's each of the a piece of this business, and any business that I've had the benefit to take a shot at or as a major aspect of.

- This is absolutely in your hands now, I can't influence you to do anything from this end, so know about what you're doing constantly. Know about when you come up against a deterrent, overcome it, learn and proceed onward, quick.

- Moving on to address number seven. How are individuals making 20k+ every month? I can't get close to that figure. Another central issue. There are so

a wide range of angles and approaches to be effective, there isn't only one technique or key to progress. The one thing that they all have, in any case, is assets and use.

- The enormous thing that you'll discover the greater part of these individuals are missing is the use, and the labor. Next time somebody makes this inquiry (if they never have, they more than likely will do later on when you begin propelling your very own items, particularly in the marketing field) ask them what they're doing to advance. E-zines will come the answer, ensured hits, hit trades. This isn't the method for the educated online advertiser, they know superior to this.

- This integrates with prior areas when we discussed getting things done without anyone else. Suppose that you've pursued this manual for the letter up until now, and will keep on doing as such through the majority of the manuals to the end. What do you have that these individuals with their paid advertisements and buys don't have? It's the use. When you complete such a framework and begin putting your sensors out, making contacts and pulling in members, you're likewise carrying with you a hell of a great deal of advancement control as far as the quantity of individuals advancing for you.

- Let me make another inquiry. If I were to disclose to you that you needed to make twenty thousand per month, for instance, and you have a half year to accomplish that status, but need to utilize standardized publicizing strategies. No joint endeavors, no offshoots, no new contacts and so on. How might you do it? More to the point would you need to do it in any case, since when you take a gander at how things ought to be done, it's far less demanding to understand why individuals fizzle and keep on falling flat, while those of us who understand this keep on prevailing again and again.

- Let's take a gander at this another way. Envision you're acquiring a thousand dollars for every month through your advancement, at around five hours per day. Your objective profit are 30k every month. At your current level you would need to work 150 hours every day to achieve that objective. That is the reason this is so essential to understand on the grounds that the numbers simply don't indicate anything humanly conceivable by one single individual.

- Just on the grounds that it's your own business, it doesn't mean you're the special case that will advance it. This my companions, is the way the huge folks profit, when numerically, taking a gander at it from a sole brokers perspective, it looks relatively unthinkable. I guarantee you, it's most certainly not. Understand this and you'll begin to perceive any reason why, and all the more essentially, how you can apply this to your business.

- Question Eight. You continue discussing joint endeavors but I can't score any, what gives? If you're experiencing difficulty pulling any joint endeavors, the principal thing that you should take a gander at is who you're reaching and what you're reaching them about.

- Many trust the solution to their business hardships is to get a cluster of advertisements to the greatest names they can get to. Issues emerge from this strategy be that as it may. Give me a chance to clarify.

- Imagine you were winning 20k per month cheerfully and discharging your very own items, have a decent rundown of clients, associates and a standard rundown. This reality is broadly known and you're a major name in web marketing. With this comes a mass of joint endeavor recommendations from individuals who need access to your significant assets. Every one of these individuals out there that see you winning such money, and believe that if they gain admittance to your rundown, they'll acquire this money as well. This means a considerable measure of week after week mail and some frequently out and out peculiar or uneducated

proposition. I'm not pointing the finger at them, but rather if guides quit advising individuals to follow enormous names that way, they'd be unquestionably fruitful.

- This isn't the situation by any stretch of the imagination, and when we talk about joint endeavors, I'm certainly not encouraging you to go out there and select huge worker from the sack, get in touch with them and attempt to get a promotion to their rundown, on the grounds that there are as of now such a significant number of individuals doing likewise. So except if you have something added to your repertoire in the method for assets and items as of now, it won't be anything but difficult to turn out to be justified, despite all the trouble. And toward the day's end, that is what we're all doing.

- Don't stress however, all isn't lost, and there's much more potential out there than you may might suspect. When we spoke beforehand about buying in to people groups records as an initial phase in joint endeavor tasks, we're discussing the greatest names that you know as well as the ones where will probably get a reaction and be seen, essentially in light of the fact that there aren't such a large number of individuals competing for a similar thing.

- That's not to state you're making due with second best, a long way from it. There have been a lot of locales that I've joined beforehand that presentation top offshoots, those that have the enormous focused on assets officially developed to elevate to, and all through these names I run over a portion of the huge folks. This is valid, but it may amaze you to discover that somewhere around ninety five percent of these best associates I've not known about previously.

- Keep this at the top of the priority list and you'll score more joint endeavors. Try not to feel caught or compelled to competing for the consideration of all the huge names, that is not how this works. There are undeniably individuals out there making a huge number of dollars every month, much more open to JV's than the enormous folks, basically in light of the fact that they're not overwhelmed with this stuff each day. This isn't to imply that don't contact the enormous folks ever, but hope to need to assemble assets and substantiate yourself in a larger part of cases to be profitable to them similarly that they are to you.

- I won't deceive you, making contacts in any case is the hardest piece of this framework, but once more, this snowballs. One transforms into two, transforms into four, transforms into twenty, transforms into who knows what number of. One joint endeavor doesn't mean one advancement. One joint endeavor implies in addition to on long haul contact, various two way advancements and a cluster more JV's originating from that excessively which can just include, making it impossible to your assets.

- So you see, the extent that joint endeavors are concerned, it's solitary something you need to do vigorously a few times, in light of the fact that after this you will be the one individuals are seeking out. If you put in the diligent work now, and set up everything as we've said in this report, and manufacture your assets in the meantime, you may not be a mogul in a half year, but rather you will have a strong decent base of assets to begin moving towards accomplishing your objectives for your life and for your business. This is the thing that this entire guide depends on, not influencing a little benefit as fast as you to can, but constructing your assets as fast and as successfully as possible, making your life of advancement a straightforward instance of four messages and a couple of discussions for every item you dispatch.

- There's one trick, and that is if you need that to transpire later, there's a ton of leg work to be done now, or, in other words what numerous individuals need to hear, but I can't lie in light of the fact that generally all that we've discussed so far ends up immaterial. The impact I'm extremely attempting to place crosswise over in this report is that it doesn't need to be moderate, it doesn't need to be hard, exhausting or costly, but it will require exertion, but trust me when I say, the outcome is justified, despite all the trouble.

- Question nine. I don't know that making my own items is for me, I simply need to advance offshoot programs. How would I approach that? As you may have speculated the appropriate response here will be fundamentally the same as the past inquiries concerning not making items. The appropriate response is I would recommend that you don't go down the course of just advancing offshoot programs except if both of coming up next are valid.

- I can understand how cool it must be to consider having the capacity to simply mail your rundown and rake in the money without doing any extra work, but you're truly undercutting yourself if you go straight for this alternative.

- The two occasions where this might be conceivable are, number one. You have just propelled your own items before and right now have a pack of assets to elevate to adequately, or have pulled in assets in some other way that would be adequate for advancing partner programs as it were.

- The second is through PPC specialty marketing, where you utilize pay per click web crawlers to advance different people groups stuff. Regardless of whether you do choose to go down this course, it's far less demanding to have your very own items added to your repertoire since you as of now understand how everything functions and can tailor your marketing through the experience you have picked up making achievement significantly more promptly accessible.

- If you've been informed that it's as simple as diving in a heap of your money for leads and hits and stuff, overlook all that. It's simply not genuine except if you're wanting to spend a large number which I don't perceive any reason why anybody would, in light of the fact that there are a lot of quicker, more compelling approaches to do this, with your very own item. Have I sold you on that yet? Obviously you could get into internet searcher marketing, but that is something totally different.

- Finally for this area question ten. I have this data and information, but where do I begin? An understandable inquiry, as when you're given new data, it's occasionally elusive a reasonable beginning stage, notwithstanding when we've placed everything all together. Not on account of anybody is thick, but rather in light of the fact that this is normal with new data regardless of what it is. Beginning is the hardest part.

- All organizations begin with five things. Initial, a thought and a longing to build up that thought, the apparatuses you have to do as such, the readiness and foundation to make everything conceivable and a business opportunity for your item.

- By far the most ideal approach to begin is with your thoughts. This is every one of the a thought framing process.

Once you've shaped a thought, regardless of how little, or how unessential to your objective market, the most critical thing is you've begun as of now. All that remaining parts is to help it through utilizing the learning and experience you've picked up. There's nothing more to it.

- Start with your thoughts. The minute that thought flies into your head and you record it, and start to consider creating, you have begun. You'll never need to ponder where to begin again, in light of the fact that as a general rule, when somebody asks me 'Where do I begin?' they line it up with, 'I have this thought you see..'. They've addressed their very own inquiry and began as of now without knowing it. It never neglects to astonish me by and by that individuals are prepared to do such extraordinary things, and making something significant and beneficial out of nothing. Regularly they don't understand they've done as such. When you know you've begun it's anything but difficult to create and proceed as I'm certain you definitely know.

- So how would you begin? Indeed, the basic answer is, by making that inquiry, you've begun as of now. Well done on making your first strides towards where you need to be.

- Ok, that is for this area. We'll proceed in the last piece of the FAQ area with more inquiries.

16. Goals Of This Section.

- To answer five last best as often as possible made inquiries by online advertisers, questions which I see each day, and relatively few individuals appear to have the response to.

- To examine the inquiry 'I need to take in more, and even buy more aides and seminars on specific subjects, but with all the conflicting data, how would I know who to trust?. A straight answer without the attempt to sell something.

- To answer question twelve, 'I don't have much money to save at the present time, what amount of cash do I have to spend to be effective?'

- To address the interfacing theme 'I'm a full time parent, or I work an all day employment, or think about, and have a bustling public activity. I don't have much time to devote to my business does that make a difference, and what amount do I require?'

- To discuss question thirteen, 'This is my first time in web based marketing, and I've never purchased a guide, or don't have much involvement yet. How would I know this isn't each of the a trick? My companions assume so when I notice web based marketing to them.

- To discuss the last and likely the most imperative inquiry to the vast majority of you perusing at this moment. 'To what extent will it take me to wind up fruitful, and would you be able to promise it will transpire?'

Welcome, and welcome to the main ten snappy fire question and answer area section three. Presently you may have seen as of now that we've really gone past the ten inquiries and answers that I would give you initially. As I was working through a portion of alternate manuals, it jumped out at me that there are still some exceptionally expansive inquiries that have been left unanswered. I'm certain you can identify with this, when you've been supporting quite a while and you feel comfortable around here, it's difficult to disclose everything to somebody without skirting probably the most straight forward focuses and questions.

So immediately, how about we begin on your third portion of the speedy fire question and answer segment.

17.   Question 11. I need to take in more and continue purchasing guides, but how would I know who to trust and if their stuff works?

A fascinating inquiry, which will jump out at a great many people toward the beginning of their marketing vocation. Particularly as there's not by any stretch of the imagination anybody out there that shows this stuff outside of the web. With things being so unoriginal, and with such a gigantic choice of data laying around for you to get, I will give you a few pointers from which you ought to have the capacity to set up yourself a strong ground of online advertisers that hold great data about the subject you're searching for without purchasing and test, and purchase and test, which at last will just put a major scratch in your pocket.

How about we take a gander at a few things that you ought to search for when purchasing different people groups stuff, and a few things that you ought to maintain a strategic distance from no matter what. First up, tributes. Who's maxim shouldn't something be said about these individuals and their items? We're searching for genuine tributes here, plain content, sound, video, or those set up together, the more the better. Pay special mind to advertisers that you definitely know and trust composing tributes about these individuals on their locales, but fizzling that, you can simply take a gander at who's advancing it.

But hang tight, back up a second. What does this mean for you as an advertiser? Like I said previously, to get the consideration of the huge folks, you'll should be entirely settled as of now, so imagine a scenario where you can't get tributes by understood individuals that everybody knows and trusts.

Indeed, you can, in a more aberrant manner. Keep in mind how I said everything interfaces with everything else in this framework, and they all create and fabricate one another in such a large number of ways that regardless i'm finding them myself? All things considered, consider your joint endeavors. These are the general population who will be telling their rundowns, and the general population that have been on them for a considerable length of time, and absolutely trust them. This is another preferred standpoint you have, and another integral motivation to score these joint endeavors. It's not just going to frame the premise of your deals and your asset building, but the premise of assume that will be passed from the rundown proprietor, to their supporters, to your site. Once more, this is another approach to prevail without battling about pulling enormous names. Unquestionably viable.

This is one of my top picks. Since I'm bought in to such a large number of advertisers records now, that only advance offshoot programs in the wake of building their assets, that is the ideal place for me to discover, who to trust, as well as a reward, what's hot and what's most certainly not. This is the reason

you'll never observe me contact the withdraw button insofar as I'm accepting promotions from best advertisers, since it's such a great device, they're doing me an administration and they get the chance to publicize their stuff and make an entire heap of money in the meantime, controlling me the correct way dependent on the examination that they've officially done. How's that for a quiet joint endeavor? It's a win, win circumstance. I would propose you do likewise, and bear in mind to keep yourself a record as well, so that if you change email tends to you can alter your membership so you're not missing anything.

The other extraordinary thing about this is, the more you blend in your picked market, the more individuals you meet and gets in touch with you increase (the greater part of who will come to you after your initial couple of items) the more you hear, the more data you're encouraged, the more shrewd you progress toward becoming. Similarly as with any piece of web based marketing, from item creation to understanding and spotting who to trust, everything creates with time and experience. As should be obvious, utilizing those two strategies, there's no requirement for broad research or to haul your wallet out for each elegantly composed direct mail advertisement.

18.   Question 12. What amount of cash do I need to spend to be effective?

The response to this inquiry is, essentially, not a ton. The magnificence of internet marketing is that the items that you make yourself cost beside nothing cash insightful. With most items, you're paying for the time it took the dealer to finish, and the learning or the bit of programming contained inside. Anybody that reveals to you that you need to go out

and spend a wad of your well deserved money on any administration, beside administrator of your business, and data, on the most proficient method to maintain your business, is off base.

The entire premise of this report is making a reasonable item in a suitable market, and figuring out how to offer it through means and strategies that don't cost you any cash to do. Obviously they may cost you different things but it won't come specifically out of your pocket. We should take a standard joint endeavor. Let's assume you're offering an item with a sticker price of a thousand dollars that you've made yourself time permitting. Giving that item away as a feature of the joint endeavor, in spite of the fact that it appears as though you're giving without end a hell of a great deal, it's not by any means, contrasted with what you receive consequently. Dislike a standard disconnected business, where you have costs to stress over, so making a misfortune on a giveaway of this sort is relatively unthinkable.

What's most essential is that you don't attempt to do everything for nothing. Put aside a spending that you can bear the cost of for that year, and you'll see that the greater part of it goes towards setting up your first item or administration. Once you've done that, it turns into an instance of wake up, think of item thought, create item, and place inside advancement framework utilizing all the product that you procured when you originally began. Beside this, and some other aides or programming your buy, really getting your item out there will cost you only your month to month facilitating cost. ($15-$25 shared facilitating or $200-$500 for devoted facilitating).

So where does everything go? In what capacity can individuals guarantee that they've lost several thousands attempting to prevail in web based marketing? All things considered, I myself have

burned through several thousands, but I wouldn't call it lost. Every one of the aides, every one of the encounters, the item dispatches, the product, but in all trustworthiness, a large portion of what I've spent was on slip-ups. I've purchased directs on this, guides on that, how to's tied in with marketing, enrollment programs and so on. In my initial days I likewise invested a considerable measure of energy being delude by individuals who educated me regarding the astounding outcomes they got with specific types of marketing or participations they've agreed to accept, and different approaches to advance my items.

You may call me artless for spending that much, but like such huge numbers of other individuals out there battling for the activity, I was simply out searching for the responses to every one of my inquiries, and you know, I'm happy I did as well, since that much cash spent presented to me an abundance of information just an arrangement of manuals, for example, this could have brought me without really spending it, and obviously, if I didn't do that, this very record wouldn't be here today. Some of the time it's great to botch a ton.

Sadly, while we're staying here discussing every one of the appropriate responses that we've found, there's as yet incalculable individuals out there searching for them. I wouldn't prefer to speculate what number of there are actually, but the offers of information items about web based marketing specifically, simply continue coming. I'm certain if everybody found their answers immediately, this wouldn't be the situation.

So I'll make you an arrangement at this moment. Every one of those different aides out there that instruct you to go out and purchase specific items and administrations with your well deserved money, whoever they're composed by, put them on hold, only for

a couple of months. Set them aside and first attempt what I'm exhibiting to you all through these manuals previously you go full scale burning through the entirety of your money on hits or leads or anything like that. I can ensure that you won't be frustrated, and your pockets will be significantly more profound toward the day's end as well, through your profit as well as by the amount you've spared by doing things effectively.

19. Question 13. What amount of time do I need to spend on my business for it to be effective?

An understandable inquiry as it's decent to know precisely where you stand with anything, and how much time it takes to make and maintain your very own online business is no exemption. The genuine issue is this is a to a great degree difficult inquiry to reply, not just on the grounds that our organizations will shift, the amount we complete every hour will change but additionally on the grounds that different assignments require different measures of time.

First up, let me give you a case of precisely what I mean. I maintain my business full time. Despite the fact that I say full time it truly isn't as a rule. We should investigate a normal day. I'd get up, bounce on the PC, burn through twenty minutes or so checking my mail and such, answering to clients and conversing with individuals on my IM list about what's been occurring without any forethought. I'd then check my business, watch that everything is running easily, at that point log off for the day and run and accomplish something with family or companions. Extraordinary huh? Well that is not exactly the full story.

Precedent two. I wake up, bounce on the PC with the expectation of building up another item that I've either been reasoning about as of late or have begun the plan plots for to pass onto a software engineer. Well at this stage, there's a hell of a great deal to do, so I'd do my standard thing, sign on, check my mail, have a visit to individuals on my errand people and discover what's been happening, at that point settle down to make this item. It may take a couple of hours, or it may take a couple of months, in which case you'll see me at my PC for anything somewhere in the range of five and fifteen hours in multi day. That is not all that terrible, on the grounds that truly it just applies to a few months of every year altogether up until now.

But then comes precedent three. Site dispatches, a most energizing time, particularly when you've been working up to it for a long time, or even a very long time as on account of this specific venture. Six or so hours before everything is set to go, you'll see me checking and twofold checking everything, ensuring the installment framework works and doesn't have any sudden blackouts (significant catastrophe for set time joint endeavors) getting reinforcements, testing the product, ensuring the item is prepared to download and so on. General last planning work. Not neglecting to check my mail and have talk to individuals on my IM list in the meantime.

At that point comes the item dispatch itself. Once in a while things can go superbly, and on uncommon events things turn out badly. I need to ensure that I'm there for the underlying drive, so zero hour, I'll be perched by my PC, sitting tight for sends to come through and the deals to begin coming in, and again ensuring that nothing turns out badly. Also watching out for my following to check whether I can detect any transient inconsistencies and issues that may have happened but not been accounted for.

If all goes easily after the initial twelve hours or thereabouts, I'd make a beeline for quaint little inn some rest, but on the events that something is accounted for and should be settled, it as a rule must be settled rapidly, because of the idea of how every asset integrates with the following one. You may in truth discover me sitting at the PC yelling at the screen 48 hours after the item has gone live. In my eyes this should be done, and as insane as it sounds, if dispatch day goes pear molded, I don't hold out much seek after whatever is left of the advancement drive. I jump at the chance to be there until the point that everything is streaming consummately.

So you see, contingent upon the conditions, you may end up at the PC for a hour daily five days seven days, or you may get yourself stuck to the screen into the early hours of the morning (and the following morning even). I think the most imperative thing to escape this is the should be adaptable is unquestionably there, unmistakably. When you're signing on and checking messages, it's not all that terrible, and when something should be settled, it's conspicuous what you need to do, so it's simply good judgment to simply ahead and do it.

The issue comes when you're taking a gander at the bits in the center. The extend periods of time don't trouble me, and I'm certain they wouldn't trouble you either if you could take a large portion of whatever remains of the year off in any case. What bothers me however is the non guided work that everybody should do make an achievement of their business. It's not by any means an instance of being sluggish, but it's certainly exceptionally unusual going from working where everybody instructs you and when to do it, ideal on over to you being in absolute control, much the same as that.

This is the place I accept a great many people fall flat, and it's likewise where it's most critical to succeed, and that is beginning taking a shot at your own ventures. It is difficult now and then to allow up the three day weekend with the goal that you can type fifty straight pages of content about your picked field of aptitude, but it's something you need to set yourself up to do, provided that you don't and sit tight for those occasions where you're in a place of, do this or lose something, you're feeling the loss of a great deal of new improvement and structuring time. Something like 50% of your online endeavors, barring advancement, ought to go towards new item plans and improvement.

That doesn't mean you need to work medium-term or sixteen hours every day seven days seven days. I understand that numerous individuals have occupations, and others began their organizations to have all the more spare time, not less. So my suggestion to you is, next time you're doing an errand, ask yourself, is this something that I've been compelled to do through condition? Settling bugs, noting sends and so on, or is this something that I got, and chose to do off my very own back, with nobody there to guide me and when to do it. Item creation for instance, or report composing, or structuring an item, composing deals duplicate, making the main move in endeavoring to score joint endeavors. This sort of work is vital, the sort that you aren't constrained into by condition, the main kind of work that will propel you as opposed to holding you in a similar place or notwithstanding pulling you in reverse.

The additional time you put in to these parts of your business, the more you will get out. The more you stick to constrained situation work, the less you will get out. So the appropriate response is truly making the inquiry void. It's not how much time you spend chipping away at your business, it's what you're doing with that time. Going through ten hours with incidental assignments

like this won't go anyplace contrasted with burning through one hour doing undertakings of your own unrestrained choice. Control your business, don't give it a chance to control you, and you can make certain regardless of how much time you spend functioning your business, it will be time well spent, and you are pushing ahead. That is the most vital thing.

20. Question 14 This is my first time in internet marketing, how would I know it's not every one of the a trick, and for what reason is that the general state of mind of the outside world?

If this is your first time in web based marketing, it's very understandable how you may have seen or heard web marketing talked about as though it were one major gathering of individuals misleading other individuals into defrauding more individuals. I'm certain you've made sense of, that is unquestionably not the situation. This is a genuine business, it's a genuine business, and it includes genuine individuals and genuine items, despite the fact that a considerable lot of them are distributed and drawn out into the open through an advanced arrangement, and many contain unadulterated data.

Oh my goodness that when I originally began in web marketing I began telling my companions. They came over and viewed my destinations, and tragically, much amazingly, they sneered. Friends as well as family as well. Whatever they could see was the standard profit on the web

message from the feature (it didn't peruse precisely that but that is all they got) and they all either didn't state anything by any means, or they clowned about me being one of those sorts that sends them messages throughout the day when they don't need them.

Obviously I knew they weren't right. The substance of the site, around then, rotated around mechanization, and not used to be cash making specified, beside in the standard two level associate program. It's a disgrace that individuals naturally accept it's a trick if it includes alluding individuals. They've caught wind of the unthinkable framework stuff, the fifty gazillion level mlm-insta-super-money tycoon medium-term framework, and they've either succumbed to it themselves, expect it's a trick since somebody they know has succumbed to it, or seen a type of brutal words about this in the media.

The issue comes when they blend these up, and accept internet marketing to all be a trick. Take a gander at your standard grid, and crunch the numbers. You'll before long make sense of a couple of things. In the first place, the chances of gaining are miniscule. Who knows what number of a huge number of individuals you have to allude on your level to come into benefit. You'd be stunned that if you took an adding machine to a large number of these old frameworks, you'd have to allude a bigger number of individuals than there really are on the planet on level 25, to get you $100 every month. Second the items. Take a gander at what we're doing here. Take a gander at what we're offering. They're not referral programs that approach to allude for alluding. They're genuine items, quality, with genuine esteem.

At the point when individuals presently get some information about what I do, and in the wake of disclosing to them I make remarks, my reaction is simple, and yours could be the equivalent. Hello,

Amazon.com has a member program, where individuals allude others and profit on anything they buy. Does that make them an illicit plan that is just out to make you broke? Because we're not an immense business with colossal names, normally just a solitary individual or with a little staff advancing single items on single sites, it doesn't mean our items are not important, and it doesn't mean they're a trick on the grounds that there's a two level referral framework up there.

Truth be told, it regularly implies that the data and sort of items and administrations open to the client are considerably more different. Never again are you just observing books distributed by huge organizations, never again are you just observing three decisions of programming when hoping to achieve an occupation. The web has made things incredibly simple for us to get our items circled and, due to the assorted variety or sorts and nature of item, and the ease of doing this, there are unavoidably some trashy bits of work out there by individuals who simply need to make a speedy buck.

As should be obvious, in addition to the fact that this is enormous cash, it's a genuine business as well. It is anything but a joke, or a trick, or anything like that. It's a different number of individuals meeting up, and at last having the capacity to stand to put their thoughts in movement and add to the decent variety of each and every market you can consider. Keep in mind, a referral program, doesn't make a trick. With a record disclosing to you how to profit on the web, despite the fact that that expression is a noteworthy 'definitely right' antique these days, the idea is as yet the equivalent. The main difference among the real world, and people groups observations through what they've heard by means of the media, their companions, and what they think they know, makes it a trick in their brain. As a general rule, it's as genuine a business as any huge name global you can think about that is out there, just in a littler bundle.

21. Question 15. To what extent will it take me to be fruitful, and would you be able to promise it will occur?

How about we search for a begin at to what extent it will take you to be effective. I'll be straightforward with you. I have no understanding about that. I think about the procedures I'm showing you, I know they enable you to be fruitful, but I don't have any acquaintance with you. I don't know how frequently you chip away at your business, I don't know if you're chipping away at an item that clients need, in reality with this restricted exchange, the main thing that I can do is give you the recipes. You need to bolster those equations through your own exertion, and in your own particular manner. Hello, once more, I'm not calling you lethargic. I know how it is the point at which you're working throughout the day, examining throughout the night, cooking, cleaning et cetera. I don't accept that everybody has even a large portion of their day to take a shot at their business yet.

What I will state to you is, notice the dynamic and responsive circumstances we discussed above, give careful consideration to the sort and nature of the work you're doing, and whether you're doing it accurately. You know, only one item can pull in a 10-12k rundown without an issue through some joint wandering and offshoots, setting up everything the way we've discussed here. It's not strange to see these kinds of records pull in two, three or even four thousand dollars for every mailing. I can't ensure you'll be effective, for the basic reason it's dependent upon you to quit arranging, quit considering and begin doing, for similar reasons I can't disclose to you to what extent it will take.

The initial step is beginning. When you're clear of effective item two you will wind up on a job. Give me a chance to ask you. Do you genuinely trust that you will pursue this entire guide and put everything without hesitation, considering that you should get two items up and running ASAP through joint endeavors, and connecting your assets and in addition we've discussed? If you do incredible, if you don't, why not make this the one? The one you really say alright, better believe it, I'll go for that, and get chipping away at it today around evening time and for whatever is left of the month until you've at last propelled your very own item or two?

This is what I'm discussing. I've just talked about with you the amount I loathe the entire worn out positive reasoning thing. Be that as it may, that doesn't imply that you shouldn't make a move. Try not to quit and say hello, I've perused numerous different aides previously, and just indifferently tailed them, hurled them to the side, uncovered them months after the fact to discover I'm still in a similar place when every other person is proceeding onward and making money with their own items, and their very own business. Try not to give it a chance to be another person this time, truly, ensure it's you. Get up and go. If you take the data in this guide, set up everything together, and then accept that counsel and truly do get up and go, and begin moving advances, at that point this is the nearest I can ever get to ensuring your prosperity, that is compelling near an ideal score. It's in your hands. You realize what to do now you have your hands on such profitable data. It's time you made utilization of it.

22. Summary

• Greetings and welcome to the main ten brisk fire question and answer segment that really transformed into the best fifteen fast fire question and answer segment. In the wake of finishing the past two areas, I had a recall when I initially started in web based marketing, to a portion of the inquiries that returned to me at that point and understood that there were more to cover, so we should get to it and cover the last five inquiries eleven to fifteen.

• Question Eleven: I need to take in more and continue purchasing guides, but who do I trust and how would I know their stuff functions? An extraordinary inquiry that I need to cover here in light of the fact that I don't need a solitary dodgy answer to fix all that we've accomplished here.

- With things being so generic it's really not such a simple assignment to make sense of who's no doubt and who isn't. Lets take a gander at a few pointers and run of the mill giveaways that will manage you the correct way. Number one, tributes. They're there for a reason, as opposed to being only a cliché marketing instrument. Who's colloquialism shouldn't something be said about this individual and their items? Is it accurate to say that they are genuine individuals, do you know if they're legitimate, would they say they are made up? Are their locales recorded if they have them? Try not to stress excessively over email tends to in light of the fact that rarely do somebody will obviously put their deliver on a page to be reaped via mechanized programming.

- Next, take a gander at memberships to your rundown. Have you known about this individual previously? What do your contacts say in regards to them, have they purchased from or encountered this individual previously? Perhaps they've heard something. It's great to check first.

- Personally, I'm bought in to such huge numbers of bulletins, e-zines and advertisers records now that this data is plain to see by and large. At the point when it's not the site I look to for confirmation that somebody hear what they're saying. Keep in mind all that exploration we did before? By buying in to a major determination of different advertisers records, you have the exploration there to look at for yourself, and if there's no expression of an item that doesn't mean it's terrible, this is only a handy research apparatus. Make a point to check their site altogether, and if it appears to be unrealistic, or you have any uncertainty about the authenticity, proceed onward.

- Question Twelve. What amount of cash will it take me to be fruitful? The response to this inquiry, in all genuineness is, well, not a considerable measure if you make the correct moves. The excellence of web based marketing is that you have no stock by and large, and item creation costs next to no regardless of whether you're procuring specialists to manufacture programming, the expenses are low due to such a great amount of rivalry out there. Anybody that reveals to you that you need to go out and burn through cash on anything beside the making of your item, your organization instruments and learning isn't coming clean.

- The entire premise of this report is making items on a financial plan and utilizing means and strategies that won't cost you a hell of a considerable measure of money to complete. Saying this current it's likewise critical that you don't endeavor to do everything for nothing since it won't occur regarding business administrator programming.

- So how do individuals guarantee they've lost a huge number of dollars in web based marketing? By and by, I have burned through many thousands, but I wouldn't call it lost. Every one of the aides, every one of the encounters, the item dispatches, the product.

- Most of this cash anyway has gone on missteps. Moment win items that we'd jump at the chance to trust fill in and in addition they guarantee, but frequently don't. Regardless of whether that comes as dodgy aides or administrations like ensured hits and leads that gloat colossal numbers that make it look relatively difficult to fall flat. As we've officially adapted however, quality over amount. If you're uncertain about an administration and need to test it, pull out all the stops, but don't connect masses of money to it until you've gotten results. If it sounds pipe dream, it most likely is.

- I'll make you an arrangement at the present time. Every one of those different aides out there that instruct you to go out and purchase specific items and administrations with your well deserved money, whoever they're composed by, put them on hold only for a couple of months. Set them aside and attempt what I'm exhibiting to you all through this guide first before you go hard and fast burning through the entirety of your money on hits or leads or anything like that. You won't be frustrated, and your pockets will be significantly more profound by the day's end as well, through your profit as well as by the amount you've spared by doing things accurately.

- Question Number 13. What amount of time do I need to spend on my business for it to be effective? An understandable inquiry, everybody has different time imperatives and can't sit at a PC throughout the day consistently because of children, work, family commitment, and so on. I can let you know however, the time venture shifts relying upon what organize you're at with your item creation and marketing. I'll show what I mean for you now.

- Here's my normal day. It's a full time business for me, I don't work anyplace else or do whatever else work shrewd. A regular day to demonstrate you exactly how hard this inquiry is to reply, and how you may need to plan for long evenings, but additionally a considerable measure of leisure time.

- So here we go, I wake up, bounce on the PC and burn through twenty minutes checking mail, noting mail and making a couple of calls, conversing with my contacts on my IM list about what's been occurring without any forethought. I'd then check my business, watch that everything is running easily and the numbers look typical for every running content, and then log off for the day and run mess about with loved ones.

- Sounds extraordinary but there's another side to this. Situation number two. I wake up, hop on the PC and do the standard procedure as above, and then start building up an item thought that I had as of late, start assembling a few designs and moving thoughts advances to perceive what works and what doesn't. Starting here this item may take fourteen days to make, a couple of months, or even a year. You'll likely, much of the time, discover me at the PC for five to fifteen hours of the day when creating items. This by and large occurs for a few months amid the year. In any case, not by any stretch of the imagination a period imperative and you could take as meager time or as long as you need at this stage, only the remaining burden is somewhat greater.

- Now comes the fun part, item dispatches. An energizing time where everything can turn out badly if you're not very much arranged, and in some cases it simply does. Six hours previously everything is prepared to go you'll see me checking and twofold checking everything, testing programming, ensuring the item is prepared to download and there are's no sudden blackouts, general last prepare work. At that point comes the item dispatch, zero hour, the underlying arranged drive when all the principal JV's are set to go out. After twelve hours if everything has gone easily, I'll get some rest, but on the odd event something doesn't work out, you may discover me composing endlessly 48 hours after dispatch endeavoring to settle things.

- You see, now and again there isn't an alternative to be proactive rather than responsive, and on odd events it just requires an insane push, an absurd measure of assurance and many, numerous hours spreading over a few days. Gratefully this is an irregularity however.

- Depending on the circumstance, you may observe that you must be more adaptable than you'd like, or now and then, than you can oversee, but different occasions, you'll be lounging around in the sun tasting martini with your companions for a considerable length of time at once. Try not to stress if you're feeling that you can't be adaptable on account of your activity, I'm not recommending you quit it, simply get ready to need to work insane hours once in a while.

- Ok back to your business now. Next time you're chipping away at your business, ask yourself, is what I'm doing a consequence of situation, or something that I chosen to do off my very own back in light of the fact that I need to make something out of the undertaking? The key here is as a rule professional dynamic rather than re-dynamic. Re-liveliness can't be kept away from on occasion, for example, settling bugs in a bit of programming or settling any issues that may happen, but a dominant part of your marketing ought to be star dynamic. If you're by and large expert dynamic you're advancing, if you're being re-dynamic you're most certainly not. This is an extraordinary marker of how you utilize your time, and if you can pull 90% of your time and make it genius dynamic, that is some quick advancement you'll be making there.

- Question 14. This is my first time in internet marketing, how would I know it's not every one of the a trick, and what's with the general state of mind of the outside world when I notice web based marketing? Regularly you may find that individuals who have been defrauded by some bizarre cash making plan will laugh at web based marketing. They got misled once or found out about somebody getting defrauded, or saw something on TV about it and in a split second idea they knew all there was to think about these plans,

consequently putting web based marketing in a similar container in light of the fact that the accentuation is on profiting, an exceptionally worn out subject.

- What they don't understand is the thing that me and you have found regarding genuine web based marketing. Genuine items that are worth genuine cash and not only a compensation conspire that gets you a bit of paper or a situation in anything.

- This is not kidding. This is genuine business, making genuine items, pitching genuine usable items and data to clients everywhere throughout the world. The previously established inclinations can be really hostile now and again, even my first item that focused on mechanization devices was laughed at by loved ones since it had a two level associate program appended to it. So be careful about what individuals may state, and if anybody comes to you and say that it's each of the a trick, drop any item on their work areas. This one, the compact disc's the sound, programming, your manifestations, anything. Hello Amazon utilizes associates and pay plans, is that a trick as well? No? Why not? Since they offer genuine items. Extraordinary do as well, we, look. Prompt exhibit of items.

- It regularly implies that the data and kind of items and administrations open to the client are considerably more assorted. Never again are you just observing books distributed by enormous organizations, never again are you just observing three decisions of programming when hoping to achieve a vocation. The web has made things incredibly simple for us to get our items flowed, and thusly the assorted variety or sorts and nature of item, and on account of the minimal effort of doing this, there are unavoidably some trashy bits of work out there by individuals who simply need to make a snappy buck. We as genuine advertisers get packaged alongside them in that heap since we notice profiting.

- As you can see, in addition to the fact that this is enormous cash, it's a genuine business as well. It is anything but a joke, or a trick, or anything like that. It's a differing number of individuals meeting up, and at long last having the capacity to stand to put their thoughts in movement and add to the assorted variety of each and every market you can consider. Keep in mind, a referral program, doesn't make a trick. With an archive revealing to you how to profit on the web, despite the fact that that expression is a noteworthy 'better believe it right' buzzword these days, the idea is as yet the equivalent, the main difference among the real world, and people groups discernments through what they've heard by means of the media, their companions, and what they think they know makes it a trick in their brain. In actuality, it's as genuine a business as any enormous name global you can think about that is out there, just in a littler bundle.

- Question 15. To what extent will it take me to be a win and would you be able to promise it will occur? We should take a gander at to what extent it will take you to be a win. I think about the strategies I'm showing you, I know they enable you to be effective, but I don't have any acquaintance with you. I don't know how frequently you deal with your business. I don't know if you're taking a shot at an item that clients need, in reality with this restricted discourse, the main thing that I can do is give you the recipes. You need to sustain those equations through your very own exertion, and in your own specific manner. Hello, once more, I'm not calling you lethargic. I know how it is the point at which you're working throughout the day, considering throughout the night, cooking, cleaning et cetera. I don't expect that everybody has even a large portion of their day to deal with their business yet.

- Did you know one single item can pull a rundown more than 10k utilizing these techniques, and more over that. That is without partners or clients included. I can't ensure that it'll occur with your first item, but on the grounds that your assets construct themselves it doesn't need to.

- The initial step is beginning. When you're clear of fruitful item two you will end up on a job. Give me a chance to ask you, do you genuinely trust that you will pursue this entire guide and put everything without hesitation, considering that you should get two items up and running ASAP through joint endeavors, and connecting your assets too, as we've discussed? If you do extraordinary, if you don't, why not make this the one? The one you really say alright, no doubt, I'll go for that, and get chipping away at it today around evening time and for whatever remains of the month until you've at last propelled your very own item or two?

- This is what I'm discussing. I've just talked about with you the amount I disdain the entire worn out positive reasoning thing. In any case, that doesn't imply that you shouldn't make a move but quit and say hello, I've perused numerous different aides previously, and just apathetically tailed them, or hurled them to the side, uncovered them months after the fact to discover I'm still in a similar place, when every other person is proceeding onward and making money with their very own items, and their own business.

- Don't let it be another person this time, genuinely, ensure it's you. Get up and go. If you take the information in this guide, set up everything together, at that point accept that exhortation, truly do get up a go, and begin moving advances, at that point this is the nearest I can ever get to ensuring your prosperity, that is powerful near an ideal score. It's in your hands. You comprehend what to do now you have your hands on such significant data. It's your turn now.

Chapter 5
Benefiting from the Impressive Google AdSense World

You've most likely heard a considerable measure about Google AdSense (or, in other words precisely known as Google AdSense V1), however you may not know exactly what it is. All things considered, for a certain something, it's a one of the most blazing better approaches to profit online without completing a ton. In the event that you've perused Robert Kiyosaki's book, "Rich Dad, Poor Dad," you realize that automated revenue is the best sort of pay to have.

Automated revenue is salary that you get without working for it. I know this may seem like some sort of "la-la-land" get-rich-fast plan, yet automated revenue is without a doubt. Truth be told, each and every very rich person on earth utilizes the influence of automated revenue to keep cash coming in while he or she flies off to gatherings and resorts and such.

The best case of automated revenue in the physical world is land. When you possess a loft building and contract a property administrator and a support group to deal with it for you and gather the rents, you should simply money the watches that come in.

Obviously, easy revenue doesn't simply occur without any forethought, or everybody would get it. On account of the flat building proprietor, it took cash, time, and learning to set up a S organization, discover a working to purchase, set up the money to get it with and get an advance for the rest, remodel it, at that point screen and contract the property director and support group. In any case, when that was altogether done, checks started coming in with practically no exertion.

Indeed, Google Adsense is what might as well be called that.

You'll need to contribute only a tad of time in finding out about it, yet once you get it set up you can anticipate seeing those pleasant checks come in. Or on the other hand, in case you're absolutely web based, seeing cash stream into your PayPal account.

1.1 So Just What is Google Adsense?

Google AdSense is a quick and totally ludicrously simple route for individuals with sites of different kinds and sizes to set up and show significant Google advertisements on the substance pages of their site and procure cash.

Since the Google AdSense advertisements identify with what your guests went to your site to find out about, or in light of the fact that the promotions coordinate to the interests and qualities of the sort of individuals your substance draws in, you presently have a way to enhance your substance pages AND make some genuine jettisons of them.

Google AdSense is likewise a path for site proprietors to give Google seek ability to guests and to gain much more cash by putting Google promotions on the list items pages. Google AdSense enables you to gain publicizing income from each and every page on your site—with a negligible speculation of your time

So what sort of promotions do you need to set up? That is the great part—you don't need to choose. Google does it for you. AdSense dependably conveys important promotions that are exactly focused—on a page-by-page premise—to the substance that individuals find on your site. For instance, in the event that you have a page that recounts the tale of your pet fish, Google will send you promotions for that site that are for pet stores, angle sustenance, angle bowls, aquariums… you get the image.

On the off chance that you choose you need to add a Google seek box to your site, at that point AdSense will convey significant promotions focused to the Google indexed lists pages that your guests' hunt ask for produced.

In case you're into overhauls, Google is presently offering "AdSense Premium", or, in other words and, for the present, offers less adaptability as far as promotion sizes - just pennants and high rises are at present accessible. You can apply utilizing existing AdWords records, or you can ask for another record. Candidates are generally advised inside multi day regarding whether they've been acknowledged for the program.

Here's the thing you have to know: Google has no strict criteria for acknowledgment into the AdSense program, and Ad Sense doesn't hit you with a base activity prerequisite. The main criteria they're extremely sticky about is the standard "satisfactory substance" necessities, and that is quite standard anyplace.

Google AdSense says they're not kidding in regards to pulling in quality substance locales, and in view of that they just enable AdSense individuals to serve one advertisement for each page. This implies you can't utilize AdSense for the two flags and skyscrapers.(Note: standards are those flat advertisements that keep running up best and down base. High rises are the tall promotions that run vertically, on the left and right of your page content.)

Once you've been acknowledged into Google AdSense, you'll have the capacity to get the AdSense ads on any site you claim utilizing a similar promotion code, if you comply with the Google rules. (What's more, that is, vital—more on that later.)

Your revealing doesn't happen continuously, however is refreshed frequently for the duration of the day. At the present time, you can't see reports dependent on a space or site premise on the off chance that you run the AdSense on in excess of one site.

Before you join, you truly should peruse the extensive and point by point FAQ on the AdSense site.

1.2 What Can it improve the situation Me?

In three words, procure you cash. More applicable promotions on your pages converts into more snaps—and more cash that you get. Since when clients tap on an advertisement, Google will pay you. In the event that you've set up your own business group, you'll get an extra advantage: AdSense supplements their endeavors. It doesn't contend with them. With AdSense, you get an announcing page that gives you a breakdown on how your advertisements are getting along and what they're acquiring.

Google has an immense publicist base, so they have advertisements for a wide range of organizations and for pretty much every kind of substance regardless of how expansive or particular it is. What's more, since

Google gives the promotions, you don't need to invest energy conversing with your sponsors.

AdSense speaks to publicists that range the range. These promoters extend from vast worldwide brands to little and nearby organizations. What's more, promotions are focused by topography so worldwide organizations can show nearby publicizing effortlessly. One additionally thing: you can utilize AdSense in numerous dialects.

So how does AdSense make sense of how to do this focused on publicizing? All things considered, AdSense can convey pertinent advertisements in light of the fact that the masters at Google see how website pages truly function and they're persistently refining their innovation to make it more astute constantly.

For instance, a few words can have a few distinct implications relying upon setting. You've witnessed th is with "two" and "as well" and "to." Google innovation is savvy enough to comprehend these qualifications from the setting that the word shows up in, so you get more focused on advertisements.

When you put a Google look box on your website you begin profiting off of web looks through that individuals do on your webpage. This capacity to look off of your page keeps them on your site longer—since they can seek from in that spot where they are—and it will just take you a couple of minutes to get AdSense up and running. The best part, obviously, is that AdSense is free for you to utilize.

1.1 What Kinds of Ads Will I Get on My Site?

Clearly, there are a few sorts of advertisements you wouldn't have any desire to have on your site, for example, explicit ones or promotions for shabby staggered showcasing plans that shout "Make $30,000 every month only to sit in front of the TV!" in huge red letters.

All things considered, you can comfort your psyche. Google has an advertisement audit process that checks the promotions they send to your site. This procedure guarantees that the advertisements that you serve up are family-accommodating and that they consent to Google's strict article rules.

Google's advertisement screening group consolidates touchy dialect channels, contribution from site proprietors like you, and a group of language specialists with great old good judgment to sift through promotions that could be wrong for your substance. What's more, if that is insufficient, you need to ability to square focused promotions and pick your own default ads. That's another pleasant component: Google sort of gives you a chance to run your very own show.

Presently, something else you may be worried about is whether the advertisements will conflict with the look, feel, and hues plot you have running with your site. Try not to stress. You can alter the presence of advertisements and browse an extensive variety of hues and formats. Same thing goes for your query items page. Also, reports are adaptable, as well. Google gives adaptable announcing apparatuses that enable you to assemble your pages whichever way you need.

That implies you can see your outcomes by URL, space, promotion compose, class and all the more so you can make sense of where your income are originating from.

1.4 How do I Get Started?

It's anything but difficult to begin with AdSense and it just takes a couple of minutes. You round out one single online application and that is it. When you're affirmed, it takes just minutes to set up AdSense; you should simply reorder an assigned square of HTML into the source code for your site. When you do that, directed promotions will begin appearing on your site.

1.5   What are Users Saying about AdSense?

It's one thing to find out about all the extraordinary focal points Google AdSense offers, including how it can profit for you in your rest. In any case, it's something else to hear

remarks from genuine, live individuals. Here are a couple of my top picks.

•   "We're seeing this great new income stream without causing any expense. We're expanding our already unsold stock, and our income per page figure keeps on developing."

-      Scott Zucker, Executive VP and COO, Intelligent Content Corp, PetPlace.com

•   "It took no time at all to duplicate and post the code on individual pages, and it fits well with our substance administration framework and with the look and feel of every one of our pages."

-      Steve Larson, Founder, Our-Hometown.com

- "Instead of burning through cash to enlist an extra deals rep to offer promotion standards, Google advertisements have turned into a virtual deals device for us. Presently we're ready to procure a large number of dollars in extra publicizing income every month that we would almost certainly have missed without Google AdSense."

- Robert Hoskins, Editor and Group Publisher, Broadband Wireless Exchange

- "Google demonstrates focused on promotions mirroring the sorts of data and administrations SeatGuru guests need. For a private venture like mine, this is the best way to deal with publicizing. You set it up effortlessly, it naturally serves applicable promotions, and it takes next to no of my time."

- Matt Daimler, Founder, SeatGuru.com

- "At the starting I was extremely worried that I may lose movement to contenders. I just utilized AdSense on a set number of the site's pages, and I viewed the details precisely. On the off chance that the movement, pages per guest, or change rates dropped I knew I could without much of a stretch draw the ads...Since actualizing AdSense, our promotion income has expanded more than ten times, and 100 percent of my accessible stock is currently sold through AdSense."

- Vik Kachoria, Entrepreneur, Real Adventure.

1.6 Am I Going to Make a Lot of Money Off of This?

While we can't ensure results, obviously, since a great deal of your prosperity lies in your very own hands, we wouldn't have composed this book on the off chance that we didn't trust in the intensity of Google AdSense. A great deal of website admins are profiting off of AdSense, and there's no reason you shouldn't be one of them.

The measure of cash you can make with Google AdSense primarily relies upon what client needs your Website fills. For example, a site about ladies' issues can make some genuine bucks on AdSense in light of the abnormal state of rivalry for related watchwords.

The CPC (cost per click) is the sum you get paid each time a client taps on one of those promotion flags. CPC rates for focused catchphrases can be more than $1, which makes an interpretation of straightforwardly to your site's acquiring potential inside the program.

In any case, in case you're in a less aggressive market, you'll profit—that is only an unavoidable truth. All things considered, it's irregular to see anybody utilizing Google AdSense report profit of not exactly a viable $1 CPM (cost per 1000 impressions), and the normal keeps running in the scope of $4-$5 CPM. A few people are making a compelling CPM of $15 or more with AdSense. Goodness, and best yet, this is all after Google takes its bonus.

About that commission… commission is certainly one thing is that is somewhat vague with AdSense. Google doesn't expose it's "cut", and just shows the distributer's cut in exclusive part reports, so getting great, exact data on this has been troublesome.

To date, examinations of AdWords rates with AdSense profit indicate commissions of somewhere in the range of 40% and 60%. Individuals guess all the time on client loads up regarding why Google declines to distribute its bonus rates, yet nobody has the appropriate response. It may have something to do with lawful reasons or it could simply be that Google needs to hold the capacity to change rates without conveying a declaration about it each time, which costs cash.

2 Building Content-Rich Sites

For one thing, for what reason would you need to manufacture content-rich sites? The short answer is "On the grounds that it keeps individuals on your site for a short time, it makes them return, and they inform their companions concerning that site."

Be that as it may, why? All things considered, for a certain something, individuals will remain on a substance rich site since it takes for a little while to peruse an article or two. Hence, while they're perusing the material, their fringe vision (off to the sides) sees little promotions that happen to encompass that articles.

Furthermore, if individuals begin to understand that a specific site has great substance that they like, and specifically, unique substance that continually changes and is refreshed, at that point they'll return to perceive what's new.

The most exceedingly bad thing on the planet to have is a stale site that never shows signs of change. Individuals will visit it precisely twice—the first run through to look at it, and the second one to perceive what's changed—and when they discover it hasn't transformed, they in all likelihood won't return. Ever.

2.1 What are Content-Rich Sites and Why Have One?

A substance rich site is one that has bunches of useful articles up at it, typically based on a subject. Most locales can't exactly pull off being WikiPedia, so they practice. For example, you could complete a site for puppy proprietors. Conceivable articles on that site would cover:

- How to make sense of what sort of puppy you need

- Where to get a pooch

- How to manage a doggie

- Life phases of a pooch

- House-preparing young doggies

- Dog preparing

- What to sustain mutts

- Whether to get in excess of one puppy

- How to mingle mutts with different pooches and with felines

- Exercise needs of mutts

- Training puppies to do traps

- Treating bugs

- Common puppy diseases and when to go to the vet

- Dog nourishment

- Taking your puppy on an excursion

- Getting a pet sitter or boarding your canine on the off chance that you don't take him on an outing

The articles you'll need to have on your site ought to be short enough with the goal that somebody can peruse them in around 5 minutes. This implies you need to stick to articles of 250 to 750 words, with 300 to 600 words ideal. To give you a thought, a solitary page in a distributed novel has around 300 words.

Obviously, your genuine reason in setting up all these pleasant minimal short articles and transforming them out every now and again isn't to simply put data out into the world. It is to have a site that individuals will return to so they will see the Google AdSense promotions, and tap on them, and afterward you will get checks via the post office.

That is a key point, so I will rehash it:

The reason for having a substance rich site is to draw in individuals to it, over and over, with the goal that they will see the advertisements and tap on them.

You may believe it's bunches of cool illustrations and hues that make a site appealing to a guest, yet it's extremely the substance. With the end goal to profit from Google AdSense, you have to get a handle on that idea. Trust me, you could run a superb publicizing effort and build up a wide range of viral showcasing apparatuses and appealing subsidiary projects.

In any case, except if your Website is content-rich, the movement spikes that you get for your endeavors may be impermanent. The specific most ideal approach to draw in and hold an online gathering of people is to give content that is helpful, significant, enlightening, instructive or simply out and out interesting as hellfire or engaging somehow.

What does a substance rich site resemble? Here are a couple of precedents.

2.2 How Do I Build One?

I know the thought of making your own one of a kind substance rich site may be a bit of scaring, yet you can do it. It's not hard. You don't need to be a decent write to have great substance on your site. Truth be told, you don't need to be an author by any means. There are a lot of fruitful individuals who profit from Google AdSense and they don't compose an expression of that substance. We'll speak more about that later, however you can procure scholars, or have visitor authors—it's not hard.

Anybody can make a substance rich Website by following a couple of key focuses:

- Have some order—keep up your site.

- Update that site regularly. Having a calendar is ideal.

- Be ready to ask, get, or commission content

Control is vital

To make a substance rich Website, you have to sharpen your concentration and your self-restraint. I don't need to disclose to you how amazingly simple it is to squander hours, even days, simply surfing around the web starting with one webpage then onto the next. You can't give yourself a chance to get occupied that way or you won't achieve anything. Begin with setting a point of confinement to surfing for entertainment only so you restrict your hunts to locales and assets that are relate specifically to your site's subject.

Order additionally applies to making creation.

Fruitful authors can't stand to sit tight for motivation to strike before beginning work. Rather, they build up a composition plan for themselves and they stay with it like it was their activity—since it is. As one renowned author stated, "I compose when I have a feeling that it. Furthermore, every morning at 9am, I make beyond any doubt I have an inclination that it." Schedule a period for yourself to take a seat at your work area and compose.

What's more, you'll have to build up another calendar for when to add substance to your Website, and pursue that timetable religiously. Make a pledge to yourself and finish it.

What's more, recollect—in the event that you essentially can't compose, or you wind up coming up with an excessive number of reasons not to compose content, simply procure somebody.

Go to Elance.com and post an undertaking to compose 20 articles of 300-600 words each for $5 to $10 each. You'll see somebody.

Normal updates are basic to your site

Nothing is deader than a site that resembles someone's disregarded it. Frequently refreshing or changing your site content gives you a major favorable position over the opposition. Web surfers will continue returning to your webpage on the off chance that they see that there's continually something new to see, learn, or appreciate each time.

2.3   What Kind of Content Should I Put Up?

Any sort you need, obviously, since we're discussing the web. However, truly, you'll need to give this theme some thought, since there's more enthusiasm for a few subjects than others.

You know the general population who are your gathering of people, since in a perfect world you're looking at something you think about. For example, in case you're discussing Ultimate Frisbee, this is on the grounds that you play it. So you realize what other Ultimate individuals resemble, and what they need to know and what they find engaging.

When you realize that, you can choose about which sorts of substance will best serve their necessities and how to approach finding or making it. Here are some broad classes to kick you off with your conceptualizing:

- Editorials

- Feature articles

- Political conclusion

- News stories

- Art displays

- A combination of the best substance

- Reviews of motion pictures, books, music

- Interviews

- Interactive highlights - surveys, input, exchange gatherings, discussions, talk

Articles

Articles are the supposition of somebody who's viewed as a specialist in the field- - (it is possible that you or a visitor supporter). This makes great substance since individuals jump at the chance to react to it, either by concurring with or restricting the essayist. This can make for an energizing page, and you'll most likely need to direct it.

Give your kin an approach to make their perspectives known; set up a notice board or visitor book on your site. Individuals will return to peruse different reactions to their remarks. Furthermore, you can utilize this input from your group of onlookers by consolidating it into a subsequent article later on.

For example, is everyone grumbling about another administration travel arrangement? Complete an article on it, since obviously that is something individuals are discussing so they'll need to find out about it.

Full-length Feature Articles

This is the most widely recognized and in numerous individuals' supposition a standout amongst other types of substance. Contingent upon what your site resembles, the articles could be long or brief, formal or loquacious, specialized or engaging.

Here are a few hints:

•   Keep it short. While there aren't any immovable guidelines, you should keep these articles underneath 1200 words. In the event that they are longer, make them into multi-part includes. Individuals hate to need to look down a great deal.

•   Articles ought to be pertinent to your site.

•   Articles should instruct, engage or advise. Try not to overpower individuals; stick to a couple of thoughts.

•   Refrain from reiterating an article you've perused elsewhere. By distributing something that is new, you up the esteem and believability of your site.

To Get Content

1.   Offer to pay visitor creators for their work. A visitor writer could be somebody you found on your release board who happens to compose well.

2.   Exchange articles with the visitor writer's site. Your site guests advantage by giving them another perspective.

What's more, you may very well increase some new normal guests from your visitor creator's site!

3. Make beyond any doubt you get selectiveness. When somebody composes for you, ensure they won't present that equivalent article to many different Websites and pamphlets. At the point when your website distributes selective substance, you have open doors for syndication in different productions, on the web and off, and you gain a considerable measure of peruser devotion. The key expression in an agreement with an essayist is that you're purchasing all rights, including electronic.

Would you be able to utilize reprints?

Republish articles composed by others, however you should dependably get consent. All work, from the minute it is composed, is copyright and possessed by the creator, regardless of whether it is set apart with a copyright image or not. Content isn't free. You can, be that as it may, make reprints fascinating and customized by putting your own 'turn' on the substance.

Compose a prologue to the subject, or remark on the creator's assessments or ends.

Take care to abstain from 'altering' the first article without the writer's consent. Maintain a strategic distance from articles that have been reproduced ordinarily before on different Websites and electronic distributions.

Political Opinion

Utilizing political supposition on your site can be dubious. Individuals are profoundly isolated nowadays and have solid suppositions. On the off chance that you do run a political site, you'll most likely need to cut out your own specialty. That being said, be set up for flamers from altogether different view focuses.

Then again, on the off chance that you can figure out how to run a site that really includes a fairly all around mannered discussion, you'll have a tremendous hit staring you in the face. Be set up to direct this sort of site.

News Stories

Your site can turn into a news hotspot for the most recent advancements and happenings in certain specialty zone by giving convenient news on subjects important to your perusers. I'm not saying you can be the following CNN or MS-NBC, on the grounds that that takes assembling a colossal activity. Be that as it may, what you can be is, for instance, the CNN of the karate world, or the ABS-News of the bonsai tree specialists.

What you'll need to do is make a different segment of your site to manage industry news. Or on the other hand, commit a whole site to news refreshes. There are numerous methods for exhibiting news:

- As an element article

- As short news cuts, with a connection to the full story

- As news stories, where every thing is clarified finally

Anyway you choose present the news, ensure you give it your very own style. Look at salon.com. Has its own style, isn't that right? Presently take a gander at drudgereport.com. That is another style. Make yours intriguing, individual, loquacious, fun, exceptional, or these – simply make it yours.

Ensure your news is important, helpful to your peruser, and convenient. Old news ain't no news by any means, it's history! So how would you get news? By:

- Subscribe to eZines regarding your matter or theme

- Sign up for email news conveyance administrations

- Register to get customary official statements on your point

- Surf the web for new news things

- Get news from daily papers, magazines and books

- Go to meetings, workshops or courses and expound on what you see and who you converse with

Conglomerating the best substance

On the off chance that you can make your site into a definitive substance asset on issues identified with your subject, I promise you you'll pull in and hold a dedicated group of onlookers. Your site will wind up known as a The Place for any individual who needs data regarding your matter. For instance, Harry Knowles has made aintitcoolnews.com into The Site for motion picture audits and advance spoilers.

Since you're the master on your theme, you can assess destinations and different assets (eZines, registries, books, disconnected productions) and sniff out the best ones to list alongside your rating and suppositions.

This kind of substance resembles the old book reports you used to need to compose for school. Read up completely regarding your matters, at that point hit the high purposes of a subject. Or on the other hand, consider composing a rundown of three separate article that have a similar subject.

Surveys of motion pictures, books, music

This is maybe the most straightforward class to get content for. On the off chance that you have companions who are film, book, or music fans, they'll presumably compose audits for nothing only for the excite of seeing their stuff on a site.

Additionally, this is a ceaseless wellspring of substance, since there are in every case new motion pictures, books and music turning out. Balance that with puppy breeds—once you've composed everything there is to say in regards to each known breed, you need to sit tight for them to think of another breed!

In the event that you need to have a ton of fun, you can survey motion pictures yourself. What's more, really, in case you're running your

Google adsense site as a business, you may even have the capacity to deduct the expense of motion picture tickets from your assessments.

Check with an assessment expert to ensure, however.

Music is simple, as well, particularly on the off chance that you live in a town that has bunches of unrecorded music or celebrations. If not, you can purchase utilized cd's on the web, tune in, and survey. Actually, you could even contract a secondary school child to do this, however check their composition aptitudes first.

Books are somewhat harder, since they set aside more opportunity to survey and cost more than album's and film tickets.

Be that as it may, you can reword what others have said in case you're astute and don't abuse copyright.

Meetings

This is a classification you should need to get an independent essayist for. Go to elance.com and peruse the profiles of Service Providers to see who does interviews, at that point converse with them. Numerous consultants have some expertise in big name interviews, and that is the thing that you need.

This is a standout amongst the most prominent sorts of locales for children, youngsters, and youthful grown-ups on the grounds that they get the chance to give their feelings (which numerous children don't get the chance to do what's needed of at home, as indicated by them) and they get the chance to converse with others.

Along these lines, on the off chance that you need to run this sort of site, remember your objective market. It merits paying a couple of bucks to an independent author or visual craftsman to concoct fun amusements that are continually changing, or new surveys, since individuals will return on numerous occasions to give their feelings. Also, keep in mind studies—individuals love to take overviews.

3. Website optimization—Search Engine Optimization

You've likely known about SEO, since it's extremely hot at the present time. It remains for Search Engine Optimization. Web optimization is the way toward expanding the measure of guests to a website by planning the webpage content with the goal that the website positions high in the indexed lists of an internet searcher.

The higher a Web webpage positions in the aftereffects of a pursuit, the more prominent the shot that a client will visit that website. Let be honest, a great many people are languid. They're not going to invest energy clicking and checking huge amounts of pages of query items. Consequently, where a webpage positions in a web scan is totally basic for coordinating more activity toward the website. Website optimization ensures that a webpage is open to an internet searcher and enhances the odds that the website will be found by the web crawler.

To see how this functions, you have to know a smidgen about how web indexes function. Commonly, an internet searcher conveys an insect to bring the greatest number of records as it can. At that point another program, called an indexer, peruses these archives and makes a record dependent on the words each report contains. Each internet searcher utilizes a one of a kind exclusive calculation to make records so that ideally just important outcomes are returned for each question.

These indexers register the catchphrase thickness.

Catchphrase thickness alludes to the how frequently a specific word shows up in a given report. It's given as a rate. Suppose you have a site about running shoes. A watchword thickness of 7% on "running" on that site page implies that out of 1000 words, 70 of them are "running."

Shockingly, the brisk buck swindlers have made sense of this, and they will set up a site that has a first page that is completely covered with watchwords. To give you a thought, an ordinary catchphrase thickness for the principle watchwords is around 3 to 7%. What these individuals will do is have something crazy like a 25% catchphrase thickness on their first page. At that point that page positions #1 in web search tool results when clients scan for that word. When the client is on the section page, they're probably going to enter the site.

Pornographers do this by setting up destinations that have content like:

Sex, sex, sex. Sex is here. You need sex. We engage in sexual relations. Pix of sex, heaps of sex.

Perceive how irritating that gets?

Web search tools used to utilize meta-labels to scan for sites. This was decent, since the meta-tag was a shrouded region of your page where you could put all the applicable watchwords and not need to stress over making your substance sound ungainly by abusing certain words.

3.1 Things to Consider

There are numerous interesting points when you go to place catchphrases in the content of your pages. Most web indexes file the full content of each page, so you should put your watchwords all through your content. Be that as it may, each web crawler utilizes distinctive positioning calculations. Furthermore, that is the extremely critical step - troublesome however it might be, you have to remember every one of them.

General tenets

Your fundamental page ought to be brimming with catchphrases since that page has a higher possibility of being listed than different pages. What's more, for some web search tools, it will be the main page that is ordered.

A few motors will rank your page very in the event that it has somewhere around 100 words on it, so think about that your base.

Registries incorporate pages dependent on the nature of their substance, so ensure your pages aren't simply arrangements of watchwords. On the off chance that you do that, you chance not getting in the enormous indexes AND you will bother perusers—they won't return.

Critical plan ideas

When you make your pages' substance, focus to:

- Keyword unmistakable quality

- Proximity

- Density

- Frequency

The thing about watchword unmistakable quality is that the best place to put catchphrases in your content is at the highest point of each page, ideally the primary page. The closer your catchphrases appear to the beginning of the page or the beginning of a sentence, the better. You'll much of the time see "catchphrase conspicuousness" used to depict web indexes' calculations. Know that a few motors likewise say the base of the page ought to contain watchwords too.

Presently, you may figure you did really great by putting your catchphrase, which was clearly "chrome", at the highest point of your page. A web index, in any case, sees your page thusly:

Home About Us Products Contact Chrome We're about Chrome guards chrome knickknacks we cherish chrome

Presently your catchphrase position doesn't look so great as it did previously, isn't that right? So the lesson of the story is: attempt to put watchword rich content at the plain best of your page.

On the off chance that you put pictures at the highest point of your page, make a point to incorporate ALT labels so the web search tool overlooks them.

Presently, about watchword nearness. A few motors, for example, Google, utilize watchword closeness as a major aspect of their positioning equations. So what's it mean? Watchword nearness alludes to how close catchphrases are to one another. You need to put your watchwords as near one another as could be expected under the circumstances and ensure your sentences are clear.

Here's a precedent:

Whimper Mix offers the simple best feline nourishment to the extent trials of genuine felines are concerned.

versus

Yowl Mix scored number one in trials to perceive what sort of sustenance is extremely favored by the commonplace feline.

The two catchphrases are "feline" and "sustenance." If a client scans for "feline nourishment," the main sentence will rank higher on the grounds that its watchwords are nearer to one another. For what reason do web crawlers do this? Provided that you're hunting down "running shoes", a page that contains "running shoes" is most likely pertinent, yet a page that contains, "I was running late for work and neglected to put on my great shoes," presumably isn't.

For what reason is catchphrase thickness essential? Since, as I said prior, it gauges how regularly that specific word comes up. Catchphrase thickness is otherwise called watchword weight. The higher the level of watchwords in relationship to other content, the higher your page will rank—to point. Many web crawlers, Google notwithstanding, have gotten astute to the way that greatly high watchword densities are presumably thought up.

Here's a case of how watchword thickness it quantified. We should expect the watchword expression is "feline nourishment."

Feline sustenance is our solitary business.

Since "is", "our," and other stop words are normally not tallied, there are three "words" in the sentence: "young doggie sustenance," (which the web index considers single word, since that is what it's hunting down), "just," and "business." "Feline nourishment" creates 1/3 of the sentence, or 33%.

Sensibly, catchphrase thickness is never this high, nor should it be or your duplicate will sound extremely thought up. The prescribed thickness is 3-7%. This implies your watchword should rehash 3-7 times for each 100 words.

Without a doubt, that may not sound hard, but rather trust me- - having 10 catchphrases and attempting to rehash every one 3-7 times for each 100 expressions of content is for all intents and purposes unthinkable.

Rather than endeavoring to do that (and having duplicate that sounds extremely irregular), pick a few of your most critical watchwords and attempt to utilize them 3-7 times for each 100 words.

So shouldn't something be said about watchword recurrence? Watchword recurrence is a proportion of the occasions catchphrases happen inside a page's content. It's sort of identified with the idea of catchphrase thickness. The reasoning is that web crawlers need to see a word utilized more than once to ensure it's something you're truly discussing. The best number of times to rehash a watchword is 3-7 times.

Try not to get excessively cunning and attempt to utilize minor or imperceptible content to put watchwords toward the start of your pages.

Web crawlers search for this, and when they discover it they call it spam and they'll most likely reject your website for it.

In this way, basically, you need to:

- Include somewhere around 100 words in page content

- Use catchphrases toward the start of the page

- Place catchphrases near one another

- Repeat catchphrases 3-7 times for each 100 words

3.2   Likes and aversions of Googlebots

What's a Googlebot? It's one of the little web-looking insects (computerized) that I discussed in the last segment. Furthermore, these bugs have unmistakable inclinations, so you need to ensure your substance is great creepy crawly sustenance.

Arachnids like:

- Neat code—less lines of code than lines of content (or a greater number of lines of content than lines of codes.)

- Normal catchphrase densities of 3-7%.

- Lots of backlinks on pages that connection back to your landing page. (Top destinations have a normal of 300 backlinks.)

- Original content not found anyplace else.

- Quick downloads of destinations, which implies not a considerable measure of dynamic URLS to different locales.

- Site maps.

- ALT Tabs for pictures.

- Link accomplices who are logically pertinent to your page (i.e., if your page is tied in with purchasing land, connections may about be the manner by which to get advances, how to prospect for arrangements, how to begin a company... however not about pet gerbils, most recent designs, or phones.)

- New content each time the arachnid comes to investigate your site.

Arachnids don't care for:

- More lines of code than content.

- Nested tables.

- Super-high catchphrase densities, which they call "watchword stuffing".

- "Doorway pages" that go about as an entry and which simply happen to have super-high catchphrase densities.

- Too numerous backlinks to your landing page from inside your space.

- Duplicate content from another site—paying little mind to who stole what from whom.

- Lots of dynamic URLs that reason a webpage to take always to download.

- Repeating precisely the same words in your connecting content, which the insect will translate as mechanized connection swapping. (Strikingly, it's fine for the creepy crawlies to be completely robotized, however they abhor it when we do that!)

- Stale content that never shows signs of change

4. About Specific Keyword Density Ranges

With the decrease of meta-labels, catchphrase thickness ranges have turned out to be vital. They've additionally turned out to be exceptionally dubious. Stop and think for a minute: you need a sufficiently high catchphrase thickness— something like 7%- - that your watchwords rank profoundly in the greater web indexes, for example, Google, Yahoo, DogPile, and HotBot.

Be that as it may, as we examined, you don't need your catchphrase densities so high that they transform your substance into over-advertised gobbledygook, nor would you like to raise a warning when the creepy crawlies come slithering over your substance. On the off chance that your watchword thickness is at least 20%, the web index will no doubt warning you for "catchphrase stuffing" and punish you by moving you down in the list items.

In this way, catchphrase thickness ranges are dubious. To compound the situation, distinctive web indexes have diverse calculations. One of them may thing a SEO watchword thickness of 18% is fine, another may not.

The main way an internet searcher can make sense of exactly what your page is about is to look for the watchwords you utilize. Those catchphrases don't really need to be there in a jiffy on the page—they can be in the title and in connections that will prompt the page. Having said that, however, watchwords that show up on your page are unquestionably the most widely recognized way that web crawlers use to choose what your page is about. Catchphrase thickness alludes to the proportion of watchwords to the aggregate number of words on the page.

Presently I need you to take a gander at the section above. There are 95 words aggregate, and I utilized "watchwords" precisely five times. The catchphrase proportion for the section, at that point, is 5 isolated by 95 times 100, or around 5.26%. Easy math, amend? You wager.

Yet, what amount does that stuff make a difference?

Indeed, it is anything but an incomprehensibly important issue, however it's entirely critical. When a web index analyzes two pages to make sense of which one should rank higher, catchphrase thickness will factor into it—typically pretty altogether. Truth be told, every other factor being equivalent (or, in other words unthinkable, yet how about we imagine), the page with the higher catchphrase thickness will for the most part rank higher.

Be that as it may, basic as Keyword Density seems to be, it can likewise get extremely unpredictable in a rush. Do plurals or other stemmed varieties of your catchphrase consider watchwords? Should stop words, which are those regular words you see all the time like "an" or "the," be disregarded while figuring thickness?

Would it be a good idea for you to incorporate off-page content, as meta labels and titles, in your estimations? Shouldn't something be said about watchword recurrence or catchphrase closeness or catchphrase noticeable quality? What's more, similar to I've said previously, remember that if your watchword thickness gets too high, web indexes very well might understand it and punish your page.

In any case, now, hang on. Despite the fact that catchphrase densities are getting the opportunity to be a mind boggling science with bunches of confused calculations, you can do it!

Watchword densities truly are not advanced science, so don't fall into the device of making things more convoluted than they should be. Go to Google and inquiry on "catchphrase thickness." The initial three pages ought to be ones that give around 20 or 25 unique apparatuses for computing KWD.

Presently you should simply pick one that feels easy to understand to you and utilize it to enhance your page, taking note of the outcomes. Presently take a stab at something unique: run a Google seek on your watchword, and run the investigation on the initial ten destinations. Investigate the outcomes. From this, you ought to get a smart thought how your page will contrast and the ten best positioning pages in Google, at any rate as far as watchword thickness.

Here's the thing that baffles individuals, however: in the event that you run and do that with three or four distinctive KWD instruments, you will no uncertainty think of various numbers, yet the chart of those numbers will look fundamentally the same as. Try not to stress over it, in light of the fact that the numbers aren't the most vital thing. You just consideration how they contrast with one another.

Something different you'll likely find is that catchphrase thickness is definitely not a decent marker of rank. The best positioning page may have a much lower thickness than the page at number ten, for instance.

For what reason does this occur, when you buckle down to get your watchword thickness high? It happens on the grounds that KWD is just a single factor among many. It's critical to a decent positioning, yet it's not the most important thing in the world of a decent positioning. What you truly need to know from your investigation is the scope of thickness esteems that rank well. Odds are great that if your page is underneath that range, getting on page one to rival the enormous pooches will be extreme, and in case you're over that range, the web crawlers may believe you're "catchphrase stuffing" and you'll be punished. Simply recall, however, the numbers are rules you should know, not cut in-stone decides that eternity characterize your destiny. Analysis!

You may hear self-broadcasted site masters say that watchword thickness should dependably keep running somewhere in the range of two and eight percent or whatever the current numbers being cited in gatherings over the Internet happen to be. That is halfway valid. Those numbers are presumably genuinely exact for most watchwords. They're founded on midpoints and it's in every case great to stick near a normal.

Be that as it may, there's an issue. Here's the means by which the issue goes: the most normally utilized letter in English is the letter "E." If you composed a ten word sentence, it would be significantly less demanding to utilize the letter E five times in that sentence than it is utilize, say, the letter Z five times. Letters aren't an even conveyance. Nor are catchphrase. Enormous stun, huh?

Keep in mind what I said before in regards to not sounding unbalanced in your substance? Indeed, the greatest thing about watchword thickness is that it must peruse well and sound extremely normal to a client. It's pointless to get a page one positioning if your substance is extremely faltering.

Like the letter E, a few catchphrases are anything but difficult to utilize a great deal of while as yet sounding characteristic. For example, if your watchword was "grass" on a site about garden care, it wouldn't be difficult to utilize "grass" a considerable measure.

Be that as it may, a few catchphrases simply don't loan themselves to being utilized a considerable measure—like "quince." (It's a kind of organic product.) Here's the decision to be made: you can utilize a normal range, which will function admirably most occasions, or you can invest energy dissecting the best ten pages to locate the best range for that specific watchword and make certain you're not attempting to enhance for a Z or a quince.

Baffled? Try not to be! It isn't that difficult. In case regardless you're befuddled, look at a contender's page in Google's reserve (which features the watchwords for you) to get a decent visual feel for thickness.

Another great tip is to play out a "genuine individual once-over to verify everything is ok" on your substance. Perusing your streamlined substance so anyone can hear a few times, and attempt to get a characteristic stream that will make the duplicate draw clients who will return. At that point investigate your substance. On the off chance that you can substitute a watchword for a pronoun without loosing your stream, do it.

For example, if your watchword is "lounger", rather than a sentence saying, "I want to lie in it," say, "I want to lie in my lounger."

4.1   Do-it-Yourself SEO

There are a huge amount of free online SEO devices accessible on the web. Most component some extremely great insights and data to enable you to streamline your site, dissect internet searcher positions, examine your rivals, and loads of different things.

There are two different ways you can utilize these free online SEO apparatuses:

(1) If you're new to SEO, these apparatuses give

great understanding on how a site is performing and positioning. Utilize them to feature issues and patterns with your site and give pointers to where enhancement work is important.

(2) If you've had some involvement with SEO, these devices will go about as a supplement to the more specific SEO instruments, similar to WebPosition Gold or SpyderOpts. You can likewise utilize them to enhance a SEO's interior information base and experience.

Here are some decision instruments for both new SEO clients and more experience SEO clients:

Catchphrase Research Tool

http://www.webmaster-toolkit.com/catchphrase look into tool.shtml/Use this to examine suitable words and expressions to incorporate into your website page's body message with the goal that you'll rank higher. It's anything but difficult to utilize. You simply enter the word or expression you need to be found under, at that point the instrument proposes extra words and expressions for you to think about utilizing.

You likewise have the alternative to choose from a scope of best web indexes, e.g. Google, Yahoo, MSN, Teoma, and so on.

Watchword Analyser Tool

http://www.webmaster-toolkit.com/watchword investigation
This one will peruse the body of the page and give you a give an account of what words are utilized and how often they are utilized.

Since most motors rank locales relying upon that site's watchword thickness (which ordinarily goes somewhere in the range of 3% and 9%), this is a great instrument to have.

Web index Position Checker Tool http://www.webmaster-toolkit.com/web crawler

This apparatus verifies whether your site shows up in the initial fifty outcomes in significant web indexes for your assigned watchword or expression. On the off chance that your URL is available, the instrument yields what position it involves. This instrument likewise fills you in as to whether some other URLs from your area show up in the indexed lists.

Connection Popularity Tool
http://www.instantposition.com/link_popularity_check.cfm
This apparatus will quantify the aggregate number of connections or "votes" that an internet searcher finds for your site. Outstanding amongst other component is that other than classifying information, it additionally creates an exceptionally cool chart of the subsequent information. One

other pleasant element is the capacity to contrast your site with your contenders to assist you with your general promoting methodology.

Meta Tag Generator

http://www.webmaster-toolkit.com/meta-tag

This naturally produces a Meta Keyword tag by perusing the page you indicate, expelling basic words from it, and picking the most utilized words on the page. Additional weight is given to words in a heading tag (and so forth.)

Hunt Term Suggestion Tool
http://inventory.overture.com/d/searchinventory/suggesti on/

This one reveals to you how often a specific catchphrase was looked for at Overture.com. It will likewise demonstrate every related scan for that catchphrase. It really is great to use to decide look recurrence among related watchword phrases

Site design improvement Tool
http://www.instantposition.com/seo_doctor.cfm

This is a device with a great deal of intensity. It tests the execution of a site by breaking down a page by vital criteria, for example, title and substance. At that point it positions the page against the criteria that the best web indexes utilize.

Furthermore, as though that isn't sufficient, it likewise gives SEO guidance to enhance your

by and large positioning. The report it puts out is well spread out and simple to peruse.

5. About Extreme Content Sites

What is extraordinary substance? Try not to stress—it's not grown-up substance, or realistic brutality, or notwithstanding anything appallingly disputable. "Extraordinary substance" alludes to huge destinations running in size from 1,000 to 10,000... even 300,000 pages.

Presently why in the world would anybody go to the inconvenience to make anything that enormous, other than endeavoring to get into the Guinness Book of World Records? They do it with the end goal to have a huge amount of pages that will result in an enormous immersion upon the web search tools.

We should take a gander at it along these lines: say you have a decent minimal ten-page site. Those ten pages give you ten opportunities to get recorded some place in an internet searcher's rankings.

Balance that with an outrageous substance site of 1,000 pages. That site has 1,000 odds of getting recorded in the rankings, which implies a portion of their pages will no uncertainty get recorded up close to the plain best.

Obviously, not the majority of the 1,000 pages will rank in the main 10—there's not room, by definition—but rather you have a superior possibility that some of them will. What's more, when you get all that activity gushing into your site, you can guide them

to your primary site by utilizing pop-unders or connections and articles on those pages.

Obviously, you can likewise utilize them to make boatloads of money by putting Google promotions on these pages utilizing Google AdSense.

Be that as it may, monitoring a large number of pages requires a decent hierarchical plan. You'll need to utilize an administration like Wordtracker.com or the Overture watchword device to discover the most well known catchphrases. Once you've made sense of those, utilization an instrument like traffichurricane.com to fabricate a colossal site.

So what all do you put in an outrageous substance site?

- Articles – make sure and sort out them by classifications. Else, it'll resemble attempting to discover a needle in a sheaf. Furthermore, it's important that they be SEO watchword rich.

- Web gatherings – individuals love discussions where they can examine things, so give them a place to vent and have their little fire wars.

- Polls – individuals additionally love to be asked their sentiments, so give them a place to express it, regardless of whether it's only a different decision survey.

- Games – countless love to play diversions.

So what kind of procedure do you use to make an extraordinary substance site? All things considered, for a certain something, you don't attempt to do it without a moment's delay. Having said that, however, on the off chance that you think you need to go extraordinary, ensure you set up a fundamental structure that takes into consideration development.

Begin little, however leave space to develop. For example, begin with a ten-page site that stays on one point.

At that point, when you get Google AdSense going and the checks are coming in, utilize the devices examined in this book to decide the most smoking watchwords of the month and utilize alternate apparatuses we discuss to fabricate your catchphrase rich substance.

Before you know it, you'll be up to thirty, sixty, even a hundred pages. At that point you'll simply need to make a guarantee to include a specific number of pages every month.

So now that you have the course of action, go ahead!

Another incredible method to fabricate a brisk substance site is with different people groups articles utilizing an instrument like Article Site Builder. This instrument manufactures content pages by pulling articles from article site indexes like ArticleCity.com and EzineArticles.com

6. Utilizing Traffic Equalizer

Activity Equalizer (TrafficEqualizer.com)

is a hot instrument that many site designers use to greatly expand activity to their site and along these lines put them on a level playing field with the huge young men. TR flaunts that they drive exceptionally focused on purchasers to your site.

Basically, you import a rundown of catchphrases, you fill in a couple of shape fields, and the program consequently makes streamlined pages. They guarantee it's extremely web index well disposed. It is a program that rapidly creates hundreds or thousands of pages that are exceptionally intended to rank well on web crawlers for colossal arrangements of watchword phrases.

You've most likely observed these sorts of pages previously. They include a promotion to finish everything and afterward there are postings that resemble an index or a web crawler.

You should simply make a rundown of catchphrases, type them into Traffic Equalizer and the product creeps internet searcher information to bring back the best outcomes for that watchword. At that point it records those destinations and additions your site at the top...and voila! It makes pages that are as far as anyone knows intended to rank well for web indexes.

6.1 Using Traffic Equalizer

You should dependably put Traffic Equalizer pages on a different area, on a different IP, even on a different server. Keep it as far from your site as could be expected under the circumstances. More on why later.

Movement Equalizer gives a layout that's... well, not extraordinary looking. What's more, listen to this: numerous clients are stating that when they utilize that unique layout, unmodified, their pages and now and again their whole site are getting dropped from Google's file. The work-around here is for you to make another format, with your very own designs. Change the hues and include your very own portion new content. You need to change this from being effortlessly conspicuous to Google.

Activity Equalizer runs a help forum...for item proprietors. So in the event that you get TE, make sure you take full preferred standpoint of it to get tips and such. Mind you, in those gatherings you'll see posts from clients who've gotten prohibited from web indexes. What you need to do is search for individuals who are getting huge amounts of movement from Traffic Equalizer and discover their privileged insights.

There are additionally some accommodating locales, for example, http://www.webtrafficstrategies.net/cb_templates which offer distinctive layouts for TE.

6.2   Google's Guidelines

I wouldn't carry out my activity right on the off chance that I didn't alert you that utilizing TE could get you tossed out of Google, and the AdSense program. That is the reason I've recorded a few alerts above. This is what Google needs to say in regards to it in their rules:

"Stay away from traps proposed to enhance web search tool rankings. A decent standard guideline is whether you'd feel great disclosing what you've done to a site that contends with you. Another valuable test is to ask, "Does this assistance my clients? Would I do this if web indexes didn't exist?"

7.   Utilizing Traffic Hurricane

Activity Hurricane (TH) is somewhat intriguing in the manner in which it's advertised. It is just sold through its JV Partners joins.

Notwithstanding, you can tackle that little issue by going specifically to one of the free download pages of one of the Traffic Hurricane Site Resellers Just Click Here.

With this free form you can assemble a huge number of pages rapidly. The drawback is that with the free form you will indicate promotions on your pages that have a place with the affiliate of the duplicate of Traffic Hurricane you downloaded.

The upside is you can attempt this new form of TH and in the event that you like it you can overhaul and evacuate these advertisements or make them your own.

For the cost I can not suggest this item sufficiently very! It is extremely valuable!

TH is highly cherished by many site proprietors, who depict it as "the ideal creepy crawly nourishment." They likewise love that it works exceptionally well for Google AdSense. TH shares much for all intents and purpose with TE. They're both not simply entryway page makers.

This is great, since entryway pages get restricted from the web crawlers and Google, specifically, is extremely unwilling to them. TH clients like the exceptional substance and connecting structure of TH, and they most particularly love that the web indexes love it.

TH makes actually a great many laser focused on pages so quick you will have a hard time believing it. It joins that capacity with an easy to understand interface that requires negligible exertion on your part. Essentially, it does what engineers used to need to do by hand—TH robotizes it.

Accordingly, clients can make pages substantially quicker and along these lines get numerous thousand more focused on hits each day. They guarantee they utilize "Top Quality Content" on every one of the pages it makes—whatever that implies. It most likely means they're endeavoring to address TE's inadequacies of horrendous substance.

Their advertising writing says, "Our framework isn't simply making a cluster of watchword rich pages that are going to consequently forward the activity that touches base at them to your primary web or partner interface. They will really give great quality substance that won't be restricted via web search tools."

TH incorporates the capacity to include RSS channels for dynamic state-of-the-art content. What are RSS channels? They are content taken from other data benefit website pages and embedded into your pages naturally.

Web search tools love this sort of substance in light of the fact that each time a web crawler creepy crawly visits your webpage, there's in every case some new substance. Activity Hurricane Pages are additionally completely adjustable. Like I made reference to in the last section, one of the central reasons the greater part of the pages that TE makes get prohibited in a rush by the significant web indexes is that they all appear to be identical.

Movement sea tempest pages are completely adaptable to the extent the sum and sort of substance put on them. In this manner, there's a superior shot that TH pages will be extraordinary. There are 14 formats to look over and you can pick from an immense scope of hues and signify 3 pictures on every one of the pages that will be made to guarantee that your pages will be one of a kind. On the off chance that you have an exceptional logo that you've structured, this would be TH incorporates the capacity to include RSS channels for dynamic progressive substance. What are RSS channels? They are content taken from other data benefit site pages and embedded into your site pages consequently.

Web search tools love this sort of substance in light of the fact that each time a web search tool creepy crawly visits your website, there's in every case some new substance. Activity Hurricane Pages are additionally completely adjustable. Like I specified in the last part, one of the main reasons the vast majority of the pages that TE makes get restricted in a rush by the real web crawlers is that they all appear to be identical.

Activity typhoon pages are completely adjustable to the extent the sum and sort of substance set on them. In this way, there's a superior possibility that TH pages will be one of a kind. There are 14 formats to browse and you can pick from an enormous scope of hues and indicate 3 pictures on every one of the pages that will be made to guarantee that your pages will be novel. In the event that you have an extraordinary logo that you've planned, this would be the place to utilize it.

8. MetaWebs

MetaWebs has been known as the Cadillac of site design improvement/activity manufacturer locales. Metawebs is a server-based programming which enables you to make boundless web index improved web pages. And business has been great. Business has been so bravo that MetaWebs (MW) (http://www.metawebs.com/) has as of late been its very own casualty achievement. In June of 2005, they shut down incidentally in the wake of having sold out their third level of enrollment. They say they will offer a more elevated amount of participation to this famous apparatus.

Messages presented on client sheets express that the old Tier 3 cost was $500 down and $500 every month, and that the new level will cost roughly $10,000. Plainly, MW is a power instrument intended for genuine clients who really need to expand wage.

How is MW ready to charge such high costs, costs individuals are arranging to pay? All things considered, in light of the fact that MW is a product discharge from SEO "master" Nathan Anderson. The enormous case is that MW is "The First White Hat Software

Device". The program is evidently ready to "(create) non-foot-printable, movement producing sites the web crawlers completely love… "

Clients were justifiably wary of these intense cases at first, and sketchy of the high cost of MW.

The buzz that MW has endeavored to make is that TE, TH and the rest are simply dark cap spam machines that make content that is fair, best case scenario.

Anderson guarantees that while MW sounds like an entryway page generator, his item is diverse in light of the fact that not at all like entryway pages, "MetaWebs are probably going to be bookmarked and returned to as a result of their significant substance." Meaning his item makes pages with genuine substance while entryway page generators simply create pages intended to trap web crawlers.

I discussed entryway pages before. Presently let me give you a definition. As characterized by About.com, entryway pages will be "pages intended to be obvious just via internet searcher arachnids, and generally simply have masses of catchphrases all over them."

MetaWebs, then again, makes sites that are exceptionally advanced, organized in php formats, and loaded up with live, dynamic substance from Anderson's Meta web crawler.

At the point when MW was discharged, its implication as a White Hat programming apparatus was met with incredulity and abhor by numerous clients who simply would not like to accept. Their principle feedback needed to do with the potential for spam to demolish web crawler results. A ton of clients feel that SERPs (Search Engine Results Pages) have turned out to be path stuffed with spam locales and entryway pages which they see as the most despicable aspect of their reality. Others point the finger at MetaWeb for the expansion in web crawler spam.

The inquiry is being asked on discussions, "To what extent will it be before Google's AdSense group begins taking action against AdSense accounts that are utilized on pages produced from watchword devices like this?" Apparently, clients who get things done by hand are angered by the individuals who utilize computerized instruments, and there is support for this.

There is likewise the dread that in the long run, somebody will—on the off chance that they haven't as of now—utilize MW for is spam. What's more, when that occurs, everybody utilizing MW will endure, since MW will leave the tracks fundamental for Google to in the end distinguish the machine age, and afterward those pages or locales will be dropped."

Others say that MetaWebs should not be being classified "white cap" since it is a computerization instrument and that, in light of the abuse, programming produced pages should be viewed as a dark cap strategy.

Anderson debate this. He concedes MetaWebs does to be sure can possibly create spam pages, yet that is not his blame. It's the blame of individuals who abuse his item. It very well may be abused, he says, "... Especially if individuals don't alter the pages that MetaWebs releases. Be that as it may, on the off chance that they consider MW a site-building instrument, rather than a spam page machine, they ought to never have an issue."

He's correct. Any apparatus that people use, from tire irons to golf clubs to weapons, can be abused. It's about plan. What's more, my assessment is that a power web apparatus like MW shouldn't be punished or restricted from SERPs in light of the fact that a few people abuse it. That resembles saying we should boycott autos on the grounds that a couple of individuals consistently abuse them to keep running over others.

It's up to the client about how they utilize MW. You could produce pages utilizing the propelled apparatuses in Dreamweaver on the off chance that you needed to. That doesn't imply that Dreamweaver is terrible programming. Anderson feels that he is "engaging the majority with something that dodges the SEO."

9. Extra Web Page Creation Software

In case you're sketchy of what TE and TH make and MetaWebs simply isn't in your financial plan, here are a couple of different choices. These devices don't break the web crawlers' SEO runs as long as you utilize them right.

In a bigger sense, this exhortation applies to most any substance creation device. You can utilize those apparatuses in a legitimate and moral way—or, in other words suggest—to make exceptionally intriguing and convincing substance, or you can utilize them in an unscrupulous method to bait clients to a site that ends up being not what they thought it was.

Despite the fact that the last methodology will draw more activity, we don't suggest it. What's more, not on the grounds that it's wrong, either. Consider it: in the event that you went to a site and it wasn't what it had professed to be, you'd think the site proprietor bamboozled the web indexes. And after that you wouldn't stick around sufficiently long to tap on any of the promotions, okay?

Nope, neither would we. It's classified "kickback."

Also, now, on to the brilliant apparatuses that speak to a portion of our best picks for convincing catchphrase rich substance creation.

9.1 Directory Generator

As the name infers, Directory Generator DirectoryGenerator.com takes a shot at registries, additionally know as entryways. The maker of DG saw that a large number of these registries and entrances have been discreetly driving thousands heaps of guests to their own destinations every day a seemingly endless amount of time.

To acknowledge how DG functions, you need to know somewhat about catalogs—there are two composes.

1. General Directory - A General Directory contains postings of pretty much anything on the planet. It isn't focused in any capacity, shape or frame.

2. Specific Niche Directory - These indexes are vertical in nature and they center around only one industry or point. Everything on this sort of site is around one point, so it's everything extremely pertinent.

DG centers around the particular specialty index. Be that as it may, it was difficult. Making a catalog has dependably been an intense activity: tedious, convoluted, and disappointing.

The huge online catalogs contain a large number of connections and assets which can take a live individual a great many hours to make. On the off chance that one individual did it, it would take years. Be that as it may, DG's figured out how to computerize the procedure.

A portion of their highlights include:

- Photo Shots of Websites - Each asset Directory Generator makes contains a Photo Shot of the

Site itself. This gives clients a see of the site before you take a gander at it.

- RSS Equalizer Integration - This channels genuine news content into your sites.

- Amazon.com Integration - Amazon offers a huge number of items and administrations and you would now be able to coordinate these items into your new Directory Generator locales with a basic reorder instrument. On the off chance that you can reorder you can immediately begin making additional income from Amazon.

- Google Adsense Integration – Since it's what this book is about, it's extraordinary that Directory Generator has a simple path for you to incorporate Google's Adsense into your catalog.

- Google Websearch Integration - Google as of late discharged an extra for Adsense that is called Websearch. It enables you to put a Google seek box on your site and get paid for any Adsense click it makes. Presently this element is in Directory Generator.

- Built In Classified Ads - Making a registry isn't sufficient. You should have the capacity to pipe the movement to

where you need. So the DG individuals made an approach to for you to make Classified Ads in Directory Generator that let you advance and drive focused on movement to any site you need, regardless of whether it is an offshoot program.

- Step Creation Wizard – Makes it simple to make DG pages. 8 basic advances, it's finished. Truly, you can most likely entire the entire procedure in only a couple of minutes. Should be possible by a 8-year-old.

- Pre-Made Templates – OK, so not every person's a website admin and you don't need to be one to profit with Google AdSense and DG with this component. There are pre-made formats for you to utilize. Simply select one, fill some stuff in, you're finished.

DG likewise includes PR Maximizer, which gives you a chance to inquiry and discover pertinent and superb destinations for you to trade joins with. This product does practically everything consequently for you, including disclosing to you the site's PR, PageRank before you even get in touch with them to discuss exchanging joins.

9.2 Traffic TurboCharger

Movement TurboCharger (TTC) www.TrafficTurboCharger.com publicizes itself as a "cutting edge SEO programming" device. Their greatest case is that they upgrade RSS channels. The great things about having RSS channels are:

- RSS channels give progressively changing substance with the goal that each time the creepy crawlies come slithering to you page, it has new substance. They extremely like that.

- RSS channels give you moment subject related substance. Google, specifically, truly cherishes this.

- RSS channels give content that is coherent via web search tools in light of the fact that the substance is a piece of your page, not at all like javascript channels which offer no favorable position in light of the fact that the little spiderbots can't peruse them.

- Your pages get filed quicker, since your substance changes day by day, so you get more visits from the Googlebot. That is something worth being thankful for.

One of the enormous points of interest of RSS channels is that you get content that resembles it's yours. You don't need to make it or pay an author to compose it. The best part is that you won't get in a bad position with the web crawlers. Why not? Since RSS channels are totally real from the perspective of web crawlers.

They're additionally valuable to your guests, who are searching for data identified with the subject of your site. Furthermore, with RSS channels, your site is continually refreshed and crisp, in light of the fact that the channels refresh when new articles or substance is added to the source you pull your substance from. With huge sources, this can happen each and every hour.

Even better, RSS channels are totally computerized so you don't need to effectively keep your pages crisp and refreshed.

10. The Eyes Have it—So Where are They?

When you're running a site, whoever is surfing it is gazing at the screen... however where? One of the greatest inquiries for web specialists is, "The place are the client's eyes looking?" Where do your eyes go when you perused articles on the Web? What do you see and what do you miss?

Indeed, we are very brave for you, since this point has been considered. Turns out that the upper left quarter of the screen gets the most consideration, as per the Eyetrack III research of The Poynter Institute, the Estlow Center for Journalism and New Media, and Eyetools.

In any case, that is not all. There's a whole other world to it than that.

Individuals' eyes have some extremely normal personal conduct standards. It likely needs to do with our seeker gatherer parentage.

To begin with, we do observation, or "recon" as the military calls it. Clients' eyes flick over the whole screen at whatever draws their consideration. Also, what draws it most? All things considered, the principal problem areas are features, photograph subtitles, subheadings, joins, menu things and the logo on the page—doesn't make a difference if it's a decent logo or an awful one, individuals take a gander at logos.

At that point the upper left corner of the screen gets exceptional consideration, presumably on the grounds that that is the place individuals hope to locate the simple best stuff. Also, the right-hand and lower some portion of the page quite often gets less consideration.

This is data that site designers must know: when you put your most essential, imperative substance outside that basic upper left corner, that vital substance should be imperceptible when individuals are settling on the important choice: regardless of whether to remain on your site and read progressively or go elsewhere.

Indeed, individuals check a page rapidly. Be that as it may, filtering has a reason: it rapidly recognizes to a client what they truly need to peruse. Fortunately in the event that you can snare them immediately, when they begin really perusing a news story on the Web, they read a bigger extent than if they were perusing that extremely same story in the daily paper.

10.1 Frontloading

Frontloading implies that you begin features, sections and connections with the most imperative words. The main words ought to impart the subject of the feature, section or connection. This isn't care for composing a novel or a story, where you have room schedule-wise to be hesitant and not come to the heart of the matter for a little while. You have about a fourth of one moment to catch that client's eye or he won't read whatever is left of the sentence. Capitalize on that chance.

In the event that you do this, and you frontload your composition, particularly at the highest point of the page, client's eyes will effectively get the most critical information, and they'll continue perusing.

Here are a few precedents of good frontloading:

- Foo Fighters discharge new compact disc

- Barbeque meat ribs formulas everybody will like

- Tom Cruise stars in another motion picture

Here are some terrible models that are not frontloaded:

- New disc is being discharged, it's by the Foo Fighters

- Everyone will love these incredible new formulas for grill hamburger ribs

- New motion picture is turning out and it'll star Tom Cruise

10.2 Don't Nest, Just List

Keep in mind school when the instructor requesting that you make a framework and you went crazy making a wide range of settled sub-headings that resembled this?

1. The United States

a. Texas

i. Austin

1. South Austin

a. The 78704 postal district

i. My house

Try not to do that.

Why? Since the last couple of things could be beyond anyone's ability to see for some individuals when they skim-read. A straight edge is a ton less demanding to examine rapidly on the Web.

Settled speck focuses and numbers are frequently utilized in business and government strategy archives and administration designs, and you're not making those, you're simply composing substance. Discover another approach to demonstrate the progression of thoughts. Web clients don't prefer to endeavor to peruse an entire group of spaces, and you will lose a few people previously they even begin perusing.

10.3 Put web joins where individuals will see them

In case you're putting web connects in, ensure they're the place individuals will see them—not in that base right-hand Corner of Death! Truly, individuals see interfaces in web content. They're typically brilliant blue and underlined, so individuals see them. Numerous individuals even read connections previously they take a gander at features.

Since you realize that, make it simple for them to get to your connections by reliably showing them in rundown shape or by pummeling them straight up against the left-hand edge.

Try not to put your connections in a sentence or they may wind up in the imperceptible right-hand territory of the substance. Truly, this implies you can't utilize the old "click here" tradition, however for a valid justification: it never worked extremely well at any rate.

Here's a case of a decent method to put in connections:

"There are a few cool skateboarding destinations you should need to look at. They truly shake and they are very brave apparatus you can get for not a great deal of bucks.

Skateboard.com Skatefreak.net Liv2skat.biz

Here's a case of an awful method to utilize joins:

On the off chance that you need to find out about the most recent in cool traps, look at skateboard.com. For the lowdown on which master skaters are doing what and dating who, you need to see skatefreak.net. What's more, one of my extremely most loved spots to peruse blog is liv2skat.com.

10.4   Never Hide Headers

Keep in mind how I said individuals look to the upper left? On the off chance that you've been focusing your features and subheadings, do despite everything you feel that is a smart thought? All things considered, it's most certainly not. Better believe it, I know daily papers, magazines and books do it. So do heaps of different locales. In any case, that is simply not where individuals need to look first.

They've tried this. Trust it or not, around 10-20 percent of individuals just actually don't see focused features, especially on the off chance that they're in a rush (and who isn't nowadays?) They look in the upper left hand corner of the substance. What's more, when they do, they see void space, in light of the fact that the focused feature begins off to one side.

So what do they do? Rather than checking right, they move their eyes down. Also, they miss the features.

Focused features are squandered features. On the off chance that you focus them, you've concealed them from 10-20% of your perusers. Should not have them by any stretch of the imagination. Furthermore, don't consider right-defending them.

Simply left-legitimize them and absolutely never stress over it again!

A word about tables: the perfect table for online is short, slender, and utilized for information. At the point when a table is too wide or too long, some portion of it is out of the peruser's characteristic field of vision. When they examine quick, they won't see every last bit of it.

10.5 Maximize your Click-Throughs With Placement

Definitely, estimate matters, yet does as well situation… especially to the extent Google AdSense advertisements are concerned. Keep in mind how I said to utilize the high rise organize for advertisements, placing them in the edges instead of pennant promotions over the best or base?

All things considered, think about how much distinction that can make. Go on, figure. Alright, I'll let you know. Ineffectively set advertisements, for example, flag promotions down at the simple base of the page, may have an active visitor clicking percentage of around 2.3% at best.

However, all around put promotions, for example, a pleasant high rise advertisement in that basic upper-left quadrant we discussed, can have an active visitor clicking percentage as high as 40%.

What's more, that is for a similar advertisement. Truly, the specific same advertisement can have an active visitor clicking percentage of a wretched 2.3% or a wonderful 40%. It has nothing to do with the advertisement itself and everything to do with where you put it.

Another perfect trap to amplify navigate is to rub the shades of the advertisements so they fit in with the shades of your site. Advertisements that are viewed as "fitting in" get a greater number of snaps than promotions that conflict.

11. Building a Virtual Content Empire to Display Ads On

So now you're prepared to manufacture your substance rich realm and begin rounding up the bucks, right? Sure you are! You don't need to be an extraordinary essayist, you simply need to know where to get great composition. What's more, hell, it truly doesn't need to be incredible. Simply great.

Here are the means you'll need to take:

1. Pick an area name – this requires some idea, since despite the fact that it's not as basic as it used to be to have an appealing space name, regardless it makes a difference to a few clients. Once you've picked one, check with http://www.web.com, or http://www.whois.net to check whether it's accessible. On the off chance that your most loved decision isn't accessible in .com arrange, consider being adaptable and having it in .net, .business, .organization, or some other shape.

2. Reserve the area name. Web.com and many, numerous others offer that administration.

3. Get web facilitating. You'll need to look around on this one, since costs and administrations and terms and conditions differ significantly.

4. Set up your new area, including your email addresses.

5. Design your site, and begin building pages.

6. Get some substance. On the off chance that you would prefer not to compose it yourself, look at:

- http://www.ezinearticles.com

- http://www.goarticles.com

- http://www.freshcontent.net/

- http://www.elance.com to procure an independent essayist who will compose articles for you. Peruse venture postings first to perceive what other individuals more often than not request these articles—they are exceptionally well known.

- ArticleSiteBuilder.com assembles your article locales naturally!

7. For great RSS channels, look at:

- http://www.rsscontentbuilder.com/

- http://www.feedster.com/

8.   Sign up with Google AdSense

9.   Update substance in any event week by week

10. Go to post box, get checks.

11.1 Blogging

"Blog" is web shorthand for "web log." They're similar to online journals. In contrast to a genuine journal, be that as it may, the whole world gets the chance to peruse them.

You ought to genuinely investigate keeping a blog, or welcoming others to blog on your webpage. Blogging is one of the most sizzling new types of substance, and numerous perusers discover it decidedly addictive. Truth be told, it's developed so quick that numerous conventional news sources, for example, daily papers and TV stations are seeing an expansion in declining perusers and watchers (it was at that point declining because of the web, yet it deteriorated) in light of the fact that clients are discovering they can go on the web and read a correspondent's close to home blog, which frequently gives delicious subtle elements that are not revealed in formal news stories.

11.2 Blog and Ping—not simply interesting names

A portion of the exceptionally greatest trendy expressions on the web right presently are Blogging and Pinging. Numerous web masters guarantee these are the basics for pulling in guests to your website and importantly making those bucks through AdSense.

The best sort of blog gives perusers a chance to put in their 2 pennies worth. Individuals love to have the capacity to voice their conclusions, and have a tendency to get disappointed when they can't. Along these lines, the best blog is an online discourse site that permits both you the web proprietor and your perusers to voice their suppositions on a particular subject.

So where do you start? All things considered, for a certain something, your blog should be particular to succeed, except if you're a VIP. Individuals will go to Paris Hilton's site to peruse pretty much any trick thing she discounts the highest point of her head, however don't figure you can do that. I know it's not reasonable, but rather that is the manner by which it is.

In case you're not acclaimed, you have to center around a specialty topic. For occasion instead of run a Blog on pooches why not have practical experience in dark labs or some other breed? I promise you, on the off chance that you put an adorable image of a dark lab with a red handkerchief around her neck up, you'll have all the other dark lab proprietors dropping by to recount anecdotes about their very own pooches.

Pinging, is the means by which you tell the whole Blog people group all in all that your Blog website is up and running. Most Blog programming has a component that does this for you when another post or remark has been made.

To put Blog programming individually server and running it freely on your website, I have observed Wordpress to be magnificent programming and this can be downloaded at http://www.wordpress.org

12. Utilizing RSS Feeds for Content

We live in the data age, and there's simply no getting around it. Data and news happens each and every day, and adroit site surfers will anticipate that you will refresh your substance consistently. Truth be told, they'd incline toward you to do that day by day, or even hourly. Also, yes—I mean day in and day out hours.

However, you gotta rest, isn't that so? What's more, have some time off every so often. So as opposed to spending each waking hour determinedly surfing around from site to site searching for substance, wouldn't you lean toward it to be gushed in to your site? Well now you can, on account of an extremely sharp administration, RSS.

RSS works so well that a great deal of site proprietors swear it remains for 'Extremely Simple Syndication'. For what reason is it basic? Since you simply select the substance you like and have it conveyed specifically to your site.

In case you're a bustling individual—and who isn't, nowadays—RSS channels can remove the problem from remaining avant-garde, by spilling in the simple most recent data that you are keen on.

So where do you get this well done? Indeed, if it's news you need, the majority of the significant news destinations give it since it is developing quickly in prominence. A couple of news

administrations that give it are Guardian, New York Times and CNN.

12.1 How do I begin utilizing RSS channels?

Indeed, the principal thing you're going to require is a news peruser. There are a wide range of renditions of these, some of which are gotten to utilizing a program, and some of which are downloadable applications. All enable you to show and buy in to the RSS channels you need.

My best picks for news perusers, recorded by the working framework they work with, are:

1. Mac OS X: NetNewsWire This is a basic yet rich Mac-like aggregator that any one can utilize, yet it's great.

2. Windows: SharpReader An extremely basic instrument, however it conveys the products.

3. Linux: Straw The best extremely aggregator for GNOME.

4. Web: Bloglines Enough said.

Presently, after you've picked a news peruser, you should simply to choose what content you need. For instance, on the off chance that you might want the most recent BBC News Entertainment stories, just visit the Entertainment segment and you will see an orange RSS catch on the left hand side.

On the off chance that you tap on the RSS catch you can buy in to the channel in different ways: you can either drag the URL of the RSS channel into your news peruser, or you can reorder the URL into another channel in your news peruser.

A few programs, including Firefox, Opera and Safari, have usefulness that naturally gets RSS channels for you. To ensure, check the subtle elements on the homesites of those programs.

RSS channels are an incredible method to get free substance gushing onto your pages.

The main drawback is that a large portion of the free RSS channels are news-arranged or stimulation situated, so on the off chance that you run, say, a site that spotlights on the most recent computer games,

your gathering of people may not by any means care that they can get the most recent news spilling in there.

To the extent the quick and dirty, each RSS channel can contain up to 15 things and is effectively parsed utilizing Perl or other open source programming. In the event that you need more points of interest, I recommend you look at Jonathan Eisenzopf's brilliant article in the February issue of Web Techniques.

Be that as it may, you don't generally need to stress excessively over the points of interest, since a basic Google look on "free open source RSS channel contents" will deliver the code you have to make your own RSS channel.

The following stage, once you've made and approved your RSS content record, is to enroll it at the different aggregators, and begin watching your movement truly spike. This happens in light of the fact that now any site can snatch and show your feed frequently, which will drive movement straight to your site.

It improves—on the off chance that you refresh your RSS record, all the outside locales that buy in to your channel will be naturally refreshed. What could be less demanding, other than viewing those pleasant, fat checks from your Google

AdSense promotions come in? All things considered, on the off chance that you utilize RSS channels, they'll cooperate!

Summing Up

With the goal that you will have them helpful as an edge of reference, you'll need to bookmark the Google Guidelines for their web crawler: http://www.google.com/website admins/guidelines.html/

To get you on your way, here's a convenient rundown of tips for utilizing AdSense:

Profiting with AdSense - Tip #1: Start now!

It's as simple as tumbling off a log to producing income with Google AdSense. After you're acknowledged to the program, simply include a couple of lines of html code to your site (Google demonstrates to you how once you're acknowledged) - and voila!

Inside a couple of minutes, your site will start showing AdWords, thus you can begin profiting. Every day you hold up means you don't make the bucks you could. So begin now.

Profiting with AdSense - Tip #2:

Make content pages for your site - and put AdWords on them.

Expecting your page is a better than average one, the more pages you have showing AdWords, the more cash you'll procure.

On the off chance that you as of now have a site, show AdWords on more pages.

Also, dependably, dependably, dependably center around making more incredible substance pages. I propose that you spending time every week for making pages (and destinations) on themes you cherish.

You'll discover more on making AdSense content pages in Tip #8.

What's more, it's particularly great if these substance pages are plainly engaged. At that point, Google will have the capacity to serve exceedingly applicable AdWords to your clients. This implies your guests will be more keen on the advertisements, which results in higher navigate rates - and more cash for you!

Profiting with AdSense - Tip #3: Whenever you can, utilize higher paying catchphrases.

Clearly, you'll gain progressively if the normal AdWord that Google shows pays more per click.

The inquiry is: how would you inspire Google to show

higher paying watchwords?

All things considered, for a certain something, don't get insatiable and make pages on random watchwords since they pay more. As such, don't make a page on 'PDA anticipates' your bike tire site since 'PDA designs' pays more than `motorcycle tires.'

How to discover which catchphrases pay best? In case you're a Google AdWords sponsor, you can sign into your AdWords record and investigation.

In case you're not an AdWords sponsor, utilize a free instrument at the compensation per-click web index, Overture.

Suggestion's device gives you a chance to perceive what promoters are paying on Overture for every catchphrase. Indeed, Overture and Google don't pay the equivalent. In any case, they're not too unique, and this device can give you a general thought of which watchwords will pay more than others.

(Additionally, don't' overlook Google's bonus, so you need to take into consideration their cut on the sum a sponsor pays for each snap.)

Profiting with AdSense - Tip #4:

You need to make new pages with higher paying catchphrases (while keeping it genuine and releveant).

Some of the time, choosing diverse catchphrases on a similar point can truly have any kind of effect in income.

Imagine you have a planting site and you need to make some new pages.

Via precisely choosing which points to center around first, you can significantly expand your pay.

With the Overture device made reference to above, you can discover that 'water planting' at present has a greatest cost of $0.50, while 'cultivating zone' is just $0.05. That implies you can procure 10 times more by making a page on 'water cultivating' than 'planting zones'! Which one to pick... no doubt, that is intense!

What you need to do is utilize data to choose which applicable watchwords to center around as you experience the way toward making new pages for your site.

Profiting with AdSense - Tip #5: Build another site on lucrative catchphrases.

This is one of my most lucrative suggestions: make a fresh out of the plastic new site to exploit Google AdSense by purposely choosing a theme with lucrative catchphrases.

At that point, obviously, you convey explosive substance on that subject.

Be that as it may, how would you know what the most astounding paying watchwords are?

Another device you can utilize originates from pay-per-click web crawler, 7Search. 7Search has a page on the 100 most noteworthy paying watchwords. Lamentably, it's not impeccable. The apparatus regularly 'times out' and gives you a mistake when you endeavor to get to the page. My best guidance is simply be patient and attempt a few times to get this rundown—it's justified, despite all the trouble.

Profiting with AdSense - Tip #6: Pull in qualified rush hour gridlock to your site.

Essential showcasing 101 says on the off chance that you get more qualified guests to your site, more individuals will normally tap on the showed AdWords, and you'll gain more.

In the event that you return and read the parts 6, 7, 8, and 9, you'll discover some explosive information.

Profiting with AdSense - Tip #7:

Consider dividing your locales: making a few pages for high web crawler activity, different pages to offer items, and still different pages only for Google AdSense.

To execute this, you'll have to perceive that diverse pages on your site can have distinctive purposes. You may have pages intended to offer particular items.

Others might be intended to rank high in the web crawlers (however never attempt to trap the web indexes). Still others can be intended for Google AdSense.

Presently, when you know which pages you're making for AdSense, your activity is straightforward; select a suitable catchphrase (or key expression).

At that point you'll utilize that catchphrase as the document name and put dashes between the words. In the precedent above, you would utilize the document name 'water-gardening.html' for your water planting page.

Ideally is that you're ready to choose catchphrases that are the most elevated paying watchword on the subject. By tweaking the document name, you might have the capacity to enhance your AdSense results drastically.

Profiting with AdSense - Tip #8:

Thump yourself out to make brilliant data pages.

The perfect Google AdSense page ought to have extraordinary substance about a quite certain theme. Go to considerable lengths to be clear about what the subject is, and precisely pick the watchword (or key expression) depicting the point. Clients don't care for unclear pages that don't make it clear what the page is about.

Try not to try and consider attempting to 'trap' AdSense. (I discussed that before, recollect? They have punishments, including getting kicked out.) Don't make a page on one point and give it a document name about an alternate subject— that is excessively befuddling.

Basically, you need to ensure the page you make offers extraordinary incentive to individuals keen on the theme. When you give amazing data on a particular point, your guests will profit and will probably navigate to applicable AdWords.

Profiting with AdSense - Tip #9: Select vertical AdWords organize.

Everybody's seen far such a large number of level standard promotions up best. Therefore, Google suggests you pick the vertical

- not even - configuration to show your AdWords.   I concur. Individuals have progressed toward becoming "pennant dazzle" to a level arrangement. Also, Google has "prepared" us to tap on pertinent content advertisements all alone site and they utilize the vertical organization.

Profiting with AdSense - Tip #10: Make beyond any doubt you show AdWords noticeably.

It's to your money related favorable position to put the AdWords close to the highest point of your page on the right. Ensure there is sufficient "breathing room" - i.e. blank area around the promotions - with the goal that they will effectively pull in your guests.

Profiting with AdSense - Tip #11: Just don't do it- - don't swindle.

I know it's enticing, in light of the fact that it appears to be so natural and it's simply staying there sitting tight for you to do it, yet don't tap on the AdWords showed without anyone else site to build your income. Google (legitimately) disapproves of this.

In addition, Google has probably the most intelligent designers around, and they are great at distinguishing this sort of misrepresentation. Also, truly, for an additional $1, is it worth getting kicked out of a cash creator like AdSense? I think not...

All things considered, I need to state that these methodologies can enable you to expand your income from Google AdSense. What's more, I for one certification that you'll have a mess of fun making content pages on themes you have an enthusiasm for.

So what're you sitting tight for? Go to Google Adsense at this moment, and begin getting those income checks!

The Gift Package

12-Step video course on how to create your own online business with 'Private Label Rights' products

https://drive.google.com/open?id=1JgsKDmeiip8sQVESCrjsazuAyPPCv-IB

1,000 Ebooks with Private Label Rights

Part 1:
https://drive.google.com/file/d/1a1sDBfPMsDzi2HHh4QsefXRbKC5aCYtm/view?usp=sharing

Part 2:
https://drive.google.com/open?id=1mh8t56784UUGx9BXsy4sYElkQpKCajHt

Part 3:
https://drive.google.com/open?id=1jssbkZWzFssn9L0cWfkvybxy9R-CC8OB

Part 4:
https://drive.google.com/open?id=1W7bsgI7KUrN38efQky1hvXRt_93XRhZd

Part 5:
https://drive.google.com/open?id=11l3Q-UMyw6Hp6iQxpuCUfRvrZ8RuRR3r

Part 6:
https://drive.google.com/open?id=1uDJ5VonWYqRaUlu_bnbALItvlEdoYigS

Part 7:
https://drive.google.com/open?id=1RSVzCim4p8BcBRjGci856DZk5ASa_5M3

Part 8:
https://drive.google.com/open?id=1Uy2DCBnqcoGdXIuAtLSHDdhIKdA6IRjj

Part 9:
https://drive.google.com/open?id=18zHuM5lisggjrj7_ecyjcRti9zzrAeY5

Part 10:
https://drive.google.com/open?id=1IaGi1QkCnuegX4uiaWTVhk-wkhhUfVVJ

Part 11:
https://drive.google.com/open?id=1FNiBgH_HXcOYiVig6z2u9zOZyd4eA9uo

100,000 Articles with Private Label Rights

Part 1:
https://drive.google.com/open?id=1X8XFj3FPDBGscf0GIPFGAHph2l3lW4me

Part 2:
https://drive.google.com/open?id=1BV4UQdhIcQapeJiNSTKn9l0kN5B_czuT

How to download:

1. Type the links in your web browser

2. Click download button (You may get this message "Google Drive can't scan this file for viruses". Ignore it and click 'Download Anyway' button. There are no any viruses in this package)

3. Once the Zip file is downloaded, right click and extract it to a folder you want

Shoot me an email and share your thoughts or ask any question: *brettsmith.kindle@gmail.com*

The End